J

"I am sorry to see that there are several branches of contemporary psychology going back to treating infantile problems with infantile techniques. This just helps immaturity grow; it doesn't do anything to help the patient mature."—*Carl Jung*

"The psychiatrists who are following my work have somewhat overdone the sexual overtones. While sexuality was an important part of my work, I'm afraid my theories about it have been somewhat misused."
—*Sigmund Freud*

"When psychology can enter the realm of the *real workings* of the human mind without fear or apologies, then we will have something worthwhile. The real workings, of course, include being psychic."
—*Carl Jung*

"One of the things I find rather distressing is the treatment the geniuses of today receive. This is a problem I ran up against in my lifetime. The geniuses of today are often not treated as such; they are thought of as quacks, cranks."—*Sigmund Freud*

"Were it not for sexuality, there would be no creativity. There would be no genius or free thinkers. There would be no great men of stature in history. There would be no mediums or psychics. All of these achievements are interrelated with one's sexuality."
—*Carl Jung*

FROM HEAVEN TO EARTH:

JUNG & FREUD RETURN

―――――――

BY ROBERT R. LEICHTMAN, M.D.
THROUGH THE MEDIUMSHIP
OF D. KENDRICK JOHNSON

―――――――

The Fourth In A Series

ARIEL PRESS
THE PUBLISHING HOUSE OF LIGHT
COLUMBUS, OHIO

Third Printing

This book is made possible by gifts
to the Publications Fund of Light.

ISBN 0-89804-054-X

TABLE OF CONTENTS

A BRIEF INTRODUCTION

*for the benefit of readers who are becoming
acquainted with our series*, From Heaven to Earth,
for the first time

Jung & Freud Return is the fourth in an important
new series of books written by Dr. Robert R. Leichtman. Each book in this series is the transcript of a conversation between Dr. Leichtman and the spirit of a
well-known genius or psychic, conducted through the
mediumship of D. Kendrick Johnson. The interviews,
which were mostly conducted in 1973, grew out of an
idea of Dr. Leichtman's to write a collection of biographical sketches which would rekindle public interest
in the exploration and investigation of the human mind
and psychic potential.

As Dr. Leichtman began composing a list of the
people he might wish to write about—people such as
Jung and Freud, William Shakespeare, Edgar Cayce,
Helena Blavatsky, Thomas Jefferson, Arthur Ford, and
Nikola Tesla—it occurred to him that all of them had
left the physical plane. Not only that, but they were
also all people with whom he had communicated
through direct clairaudience at one time or another.

[5]

So, rather than just write biographical sketches of them, he reasoned, why not speak to them *directly*— through a medium—and let them talk about their lives, experiences, inspirations, and current thoughts *in their own words!*

The choice of a medium was an easy one. Dr. Leichtman immediately thought of his good friend, David Kendrick Johnson. Dr. Leichtman knew that Mr. Johnson had been ''entertaining'' Jung, Cayce, Madame Blavatsky, and many of the others on his list for quite some time already. And he respected David's talent as a medium to work compatibly with creative and innovative spirits. A first-rate artist in his own right, David has the understanding and competence which make it possible for other creative geniuses to speak through him, mediumistically. So Dr. Leicht-man broached the idea. Mr. Johnson responded enthusiastically.

By the time they began the series of interviews, Dr. Leichtman and Mr. Johnson had drawn up a rather impressive list of people to converse with—heavily weighted toward those who had been gifted with unusual inspiration and vision while alive in the physical body. They decided, for example, to contact such outstanding mediums and pioneers in the exploration of life after death as Edgar Cayce, Arthur Ford, Eileen Garrett, and Stewart Edward White. Also making the list were a number of mysterious, ''occult'' personages: Cheiro, the actor-turned-palmist who gained much fame in Europe with his amazing predictions around the turn of the century; the controversial Madame Blavatsky, who helped found the Theosophical Society and who claimed to be in contact with super-

[6]

human "Masters"; and C.W. Leadbeater, the clergyman who became a clairvoyant and author of many books on the invisible dimensions of life. Rounding out the list were a number of geniuses who obviously had led inspired lives while being less overtly psychic: William Shakespeare; Jung and Freud; Thomas Jefferson, Nikola Tesla, the electrical genius; and Sir Oliver Lodge, the British physicist, educator, and early psychic investigator.

As the series' title, *From Heaven to Earth*, suggests, the purpose of this project is to acquaint readers with the current thinking of these outstanding individuals, even though they have left their physical bodies and now work on the inner dimensions of reality. Many new ideas about psychology, psychic phenomena, science, literature, human civilization, and the future of mankind are set forth in these conversations—as well as plenty of good humor.

It is not the intent of this series to document the existence of life after death—or the effectiveness of mediumship in contacting the spirits of those who have left their physical bodies. Nor is it necessary, for these matters have been scientifically proven many times over in other writings—indeed, in many of the books written by the people interviewed in this series. The doubting reader will find ample proof in the works of Sir Oliver Lodge, Stewart Edward White, Eileen Garrett, Madame Blavatsky, C.W. Leadbeater, Arthur Ford—and countless others.

Instead, the interviews in *From Heaven to Earth* are offered as a way of demonstrating that we need not be content with just an echo of great geniuses who have lived and died; their voices can literally be heard again.

Their spirits and ideas can actually return to earth. Heaven is not some faraway place inaccessible to mortals. It can easily be contacted by competent psychics and mediums who have correctly trained themselves— as have Dr. Leichtman and Mr. Johnson. And such contact can produce insights and new ideas of great importance.

A more complete introduction to this series is contained in the first book, Edgar Cayce Returns. *In it, the nature of the mediumistic trance, the origins of this specific project, and the value of creative genius are discussed in detail. For information on ordering this first issue in the series, please see page 99 in this volume.*

—Carl Japikse
ARIEL PRESS

JUNG & FREUD RETURN

One of the truly remarkable developments in human civilization during the last one hundred years has been the emergence of the science of psychology and its related practices of psychiatry and therapy. The human psyche is a noble creation that deserves to be studied and understood. For many centuries, mankind was afraid to probe too deeply into its own constitution; the result was centuries of ignorance. No one, however, should be afraid to discover the many marvels of consciousness within his own being. The rapid growth of psychological knowledge has helped tear away the veils of ignorance and fear, so that men and women can more easily discover these inner marvels for themselves.

Each human being has a vital interest in the science of psychology—not just psychologists and psychiatrists. It is the work of the specialists and professionals in the field to break new ground and formulate useful ideas. But each of us should appreciate the value of psychology and its application to our lives. Each of us has a psyche. To understand it, we must become students of psychology. We must learn to recognize the wise psychologists of our time and try to relate their ideas to our own needs and situations.

Beyond dispute, the two most significant figures in the development of modern psychology and psychiatry are Sigmund Freud and Carl Jung. Freud was the brilliant innovator whose theories and writings captured the attention of intelligent people and challenged them to begin thinking about the deeper elements of human life. He deserves great credit for the contributions he made to our understanding of the human mind. So does his colleague Jung, whose writings and ideas are only beginning to be appreciated properly. In many respects, he was light years ahead of the rest of his profession. A great admirer of Dr. Freud, he nonetheless broke with his mentor as he began to perceive the collective nature of the human psyche—an idea that Dr. Freud was not prepared to accept during his lifetime.

Dr. Jung was one of the first people I thought of when I decided to do this project of interviewing the spirits of famous geniuses and psychics. Although he was part of a profession that often scorns psychic phenomena, Dr. Jung's work clearly shows the need for an intelligent and mature understanding of intuition and psychic phenomena—if we are really going to comprehend the full nature of consciousness. Psychologists and psychiatrists who discount the validity of psychic phenomena need to awake to the fact that their profession itself is grounded in the interplay of psychic energies!

Dr. Jung suggested that Dr. Freud also be included in the interview—in part to demonstrate that the supposed rift between the two of them has been greatly exaggerated, but also because Freud has some surprising ideas about the future development of psychology and psychiatry, now that he is a spirit.

The contribution of these two doctors to psychology and the world cannot be fully grasped unless we understand the state of society before they began their work. In a world devoid of any organized school of psychology, mental illness was regarded as a degrading and uncivilized departure from acceptable behavior. The stigma attached to mental sickness was nearly as severe as the curse of leprosy had been centuries before. Relief or cure of mental illness was not given realistic consideration in most cases; custodial care in institutions, or no care at all, was the usual lot of those so afflicted.

Beyond that, mankind was troubled by a severe social neurosis at the time Dr. Freud began his work— the crippling repression of sexuality, which was damaging the creative and social expressiveness of men and women alike in the Western world. The frustration of this very human drive and function was a major cause of what quite accurately could be called a neurosis of society.

It was into this epoch of confusion and illness that Freud entered. The details of his struggle and eventual rise to pre-eminence in the field of psychiatry cannot be covered in this brief introduction. But in retrospect, it is worthwhile to recognize that the genius of Freud served as a focus and catalyst for the birth of a new, scientific approach to human behavior.

Around Freud gathered other pioneers of this fledgling science. Adler, Rank, Jung, and others found the early Vienna School—and Freud's genius—to be a setting in which they could nurture their own insights about mental health and illness. While they eventually went their own ways, history cannot deny that Freud's inspiration and work stand at the headwaters of many schools of thought in psychology today.

One of Freud's major contributions was to popularize the concept of a personal unconscious—a reservoir of half-forgotten or repressed memories, feelings, and inhibited urges. He explored this dimension of the mind and discovered it to be the battleground from which arise all manner of conflicts—conflicts which can erupt to disturb the proper functioning of the conscious personality. The development of this idea alone was an important step forward in the work of psychoanalysis.

Freud is best remembered today for his efforts to understand the disturbances that arise in parent-child relationships. His theory that a repressed sexual drive was the main source of conflict proved to be a bombshell that shattered the social hypocrisy and mores of his day.

Today, some authorities consider this sort of conflict only one of many causes for disturbed emotions and behavior. But in Freud's time, it was a very prevalent and exceedingly damaging source of human suffering. In his zeal to attack an epidemic of sexual neuroses, he may have overlooked alternate possibilities. Nevertheless, Freud is responsible in no small way for relieving humanity of a substantial illness in its collective body. Society as a whole and each of us individually are the benefactors of his pioneer work.

Dr. Jung extended Dr. Freud's insights into the human mind in several wonderful ways. He alerted us, for example, to the importance of historical influences—social, religious, and educational conditionings—on our individual development and behavior. He described how we each respond to archetypal images and ideas. Jung also expanded Freud's idea of a personal unconscious to include a pool of half-forgotten memories, ideas, and attitudes which belong to the whole race of humanity. He labeled this the ''collective unconscious.''

These were startling ideas that pointed to the existence of a common bond among all humans on a purely mental level, not just physically. Jung devoted his life to proving scientifically that certain transcultural and transpersonal, non-physical influences have affected many different societies in many different historical epochs in similar ways.

It is doubtful that the full impact of this revelation has been comprehended by the average psychologist, psychiatrist, or layman. While controversy still surrounds this theory, it does—if it is true—give a scientific basis to the ages old concept of a brotherhood of all people. It also means that there is indeed a vast sea of psychic energies and archetypes in which we all live. In this light, Jung can be ranked as one of the greatest contributors to parapsychology in the twentieth century. Much of his work is a gold mine of evidence which points to the reality of psychic forces and events. He also provided a theoretical basis for explaining these phenomena.

In his writings, Jung highlighted and articulated—perhaps for the first time—the idea that the human mind has the capacity to heal itself, just as the physical body has an ability to heal itself. This, too, is an important idea that anticipated the modern depth and humanistically-oriented psychologies, which hold that there is an essential core of mental health within each of us, a seed of maturity and intelligence. This central core is continually struggling to express itself in our external behavior. Jung labeled it the ''higher self.'' For him, it was an element of consciousness that could transcend the primitive forces and animal instincts that Freud had called the id.

In their day, Freud's and Jung's psychological innovations were no less startling than the first popular, mass-produced automobile. But insights into the workings of the human mind and modes of therapy have advanced since that day, just as the automotive industry has advanced. It is as outdated to cling literally to their theories as it is to drive a Model-T Ford. Instead, their ideas should be respected for what they are—foundations of thought and genius that can be built upon and enlarged. Indeed, in the interview that follows, both Jung and Freud make it clear that there is a continuing need to experiment and explore in our ways of looking at the human mind and behavior. Just as individual and collective consciousness continue to evolve in a healthy society, so should the study of the wonderful human mind evolve as well. That is the challenge of modern psychology.

Not surprisingly, both Jung and Freud are involved now as spirits in the development of new forms of psychology. Both advocate integrating an awareness of the psychic aspects of the human mind into psychological theories and techniques, and state that they are working from the inner planes to inspire that type of development.

In reading the interview that follows, it may be helpful to realize that both Jung and Freud were quite psychic in their lifetimes—although they preferred not to reveal this fact in public. Jung did describe countless psychic happenings in his memoirs, *Memories, Dreams, and Reflections*, but carefully distinguished this book from his scientific writings. One of the most intriguing psychic events that occurred in his life was the episode that led to his writing a short monograph called *Seven Sermons to the Dead*. As this piece is discussed by Jung in our interview, I will include a brief explanation of it here. A more complete account can be found in Nandor Fodor's book, *Freud, Jung, and Occultism*.

About the time of World War I, Jung arrived home one evening to find his house filled with the spirits of several deceased people. They kept insisting that they were searching for answers to some very important questions, and indicated that they would not leave until Dr. Jung had supplied them. For the next several days, therefore, he labored to set down his written reply to them about the nature of God and life. These responses later were published as *Seven Sermons to the Dead*.

This experience was nothing less than a series of actual clairvoyant communications with the minds of these spirits. Jung later realized that it was a wonderful educational experience for him—apparently conducted more for his benefit than for the so-called dead. It certainly must have added a new dimension to his comprehension of the boundaries of the human mind.

[15]

Several times in our conversation, Dr. Jung referred to technical terms and labels that he used in his writings during his career. Since these are not fully explained during the interview, it may be helpful to outline the most important terms here. Many of them are also defined in a glossary which follows the text of the interview. It is difficult, however, to adequately condense some of Dr. Jung's more complex ideas. The reader who is interested in a fuller understanding of these terms and theories should take the time to study the extensive writings Jung left behind.

Jung, for example, refers to an analogy which describes the relationship of the conscious mind to the personal and collective unconscious as being like the relationship of an island to the ocean around it. The island, as it appears above the water level, represents the conscious mind. The part of the island that is submerged is the personal unconscious. Deeper, at the very base of the island, is the floor of the ocean. This submerged land connects the island with all other islands; it represents the collective unconscious, which influences all humanity.

Jung felt that one of the most important aspects of this analogy was the tidal zone of the island's shoreline, which he equated with the *shadow* territory of consciousness—the gray area at the border of the conscious and unconscious aspects of the mind. The shadow is an area in which some repressed or suppressed material could potentially emerge into conscious awareness and experience. The integration of this material from the shadow into the conscious mind is the goal of psychotherapy and the means of achieving a more mature relationship with our personal world.

[16]

Archetype is another term that needs explanation, as Jung uses it frequently in our conversation. It is a fundamental concept in his view of consciousness. A Jungian archetype is any primordial force which is common to large masses of people. These forces are associated with symbols that may have been prevalent in mass consciousness and the collective unconscious for centuries. They are recognized by their occasional visual appearance in personal dreams, as well as by their frequent use in the myths, religious motifs, and symbolic images of many cultures. Archetypes are also experienced as urges, feelings, inhibitions, or motivating energies which influence our personal behavior. Jung felt that the identification of archetypes and their qualities is a major step in the analysis of any individual's state of mind, conscious or unconscious. It is a means of consciously recognizing the unconscious forces at work in a person's life.

Another term Jung uses in the interview is *parapsychic*. Since he had used the word ''psychic'' in his writings to refer to any psychological energy, he felt that he should use a different term in our conversation when referring to the intuitive experiences which are usually called ''psychic.'' ''Parapsychic'' is the word he coined for the occasion.

The interview begins with me talking with Dr. Jung through the mediumship of my good friend, David Kendrick Johnson. We talked for most of an afternoon, then stopped for dinner. After dining, another close friend, Paul Winters, also went into trance, so that I could talk with Dr. Jung and Dr. Freud simultaneously—Dr. Jung speaking through David and Dr. Freud talking through Paul. The three-way conversation that resulted was lively, informative, and often hilarious, as the two psychologists recalled their days together in Vienna.

I should point out that neither Dr. Jung nor Dr. Freud spoke with a Germanic accent—they each used the voice patterns that were normal to the mediums, both of whom are American. However, the sentence structure of their responses was often Germanic in nature—long, complex sentences with the verbs near the end. Neither Dave nor Paul speaks in this way normally. Thus, although speaking through a medium, Drs. Jung and Freud did continue to think in their own styles. Since Germanic construction is not easily read by most Americans, I have taken the liberty to rearrange the wording of some of their comments, always preserving the original meaning.

Dr. Jung begins with a comment about the mental processes of animals, which had been the topic of conversation just prior to beginning the interview. I had been speculating with several physical friends who attended the interview (but did not participate in it) about the thought processes of dogs, how their little minds were organized, what types of psychological problems they had, and how they worked them out without benefit of psychiatrists.

Jung: I overheard some of the remarks you made about animals. Actually, animals are working with a shadow personality more than a complete personality in the human sense. They repress a great deal less than people do, because most of their responses are instinctual. They don't have the capacity, like humans do, to talk themselves into anything that ''needs'' repressing. Housebreaking, perhaps, generates a major repression for them—but only because they are forced by humans to feel ashamed of a natural act. Of course, considering the alternative, repression in that instance is rather desirable. [*Laughter.*]

Leichtman: Yes, I suppose their behavior *is* more typical of the operation of the shadow.

Jung: The shadow, of course, can be thought of as the personality's extension into the unconscious. It is the personalized part of the unconscious.

Leichtman: In the human psyche, how does repression occur?

Jung: With most people, repression happens more or less automatically. Many patterns of repression begin very early in childhood, and the conscious mind has no memory of them. Do you have any memory of having your diapers changed, for instance? [*Laughter.*] Well, that's the period of your life when many of the memory patterns you ordinarily repress have their beginnings. They are influenced in part by parents, but also by the fact that we do come into physical life with character traits from previous life experiences. Some of these are good; others are bad. I got interested in this late in my career, but had very little opportunity to explore it as well as I would have liked.

I began, incidentally, a past life recall of my own at one time. The memory was so clear and exact that I knew that it was not an illusion or a daydream. There were lots of ideas I would have loved to have gotten into and explored, but the times were not right.

Freud may even tell you—he said it to me one time, I think in jest—that if he had to choose a career again, he would be a psychic.

[19]

Leichtman [*laughing*]: He's got to be kidding!

Jung: Well, in a psychiatrist-less world, he probably would have done as well. He was—dare we say it?—a repressed psychic. His mother was psychic; so was his grandfather. It ran in the family. Many of his insights came literally as psychic insights, and I am using "psychic" in the sense that you use it—to refer to paranormal phenomena of the mind.

I suppose that if we're going to get technical, we'll have to label phenomena such as trances and mind reading as "parapsychic." If we're going to stick to my original use of the word "psychic," this will be necessary.

Leichtman: Fine.

Jung: I'd like to make a personal comment here. I am looking forward to a very pleasurable task in the next few years—I'll be helping David [the medium, Mr. Johnson] on a project involving the symbols of astrology.

Leichtman: Do you mean an elaboration of the Sabian symbols?

Jung: That and more. I don't suppose you know this, but David has read quite a bit in my works, particularly in *Man and His Symbols.* While he doesn't know the jargon, he has a very good intuitive grasp of what I was talking about. He tends to make his own labels, but after all—

Leichtman: Yes, a rose is a rose is a rose.

Jung: I also have the honor of helping him with a good deal of the art work he'll be doing in the next few years. There's an important group of artists who will be helping him with it, too. A Mr. Rackham in particular [Arthur Rackham, an English artist known for his illustrations of fairy tales].

Leichtman: Oh, excellent.

Jung: I've always thought that Mr. Rackham and David, if they had had the opportunity to meet in life, would have enjoyed each other very much. Mr. Rackham is very much of the same temperament. He has a very, how shall I say it, wry sense of humor. Incidentally, Mr. Rackham is continuing to promote, as he did during his physical life, the artistic expression of the quintessence of certain psychic ideas. In psychology, we would say that he's working with a group of archetypes, but in parapsychic terms, he's working with clairvoyant visions. Mr. Rackham was very much aware of his clairvoyance.

Now, I'm finding it difficult to place the idea of clairvoyance into my model of consciousness. You know the one, don't you—the analogy of the island in the ocean which I used to represent the several levels of the mind. No analogy, of course, is perfect.

Mediumship, to me, would be a door that could be entered at low tide—that is, from the shadow. It would be a secret entrance to the mind. Ordinary psychic awareness, however, would be like putting a skylight on top of the island. [*Chuckling*] Your readers may have to use a bit of imagination to visualize that, but it's the best way I can fit in clairvoyance.

Leichtman: Yes, that's a helpful addition.

Jung: Of course, there are always those who have to put glasses on their skylights to see through them. [*Laughter.*] I suppose you'd better describe that whole model in your introduction, Doctor, so the readers will know what I'm talking about.

Leichtman: Okay. Now that you've mentioned

[21]

archetypes, can I ask you some questions about them? Can they be directly perceived and studied? I'm referring to such exercises as meditating on a Tarot card.

Jung: Yes. Archetypes do have an existence apart from a person's mind and even apart from mankind's racial memory. Only so much can be learned by cataloguing them and intellectually analyzing them—that kind of study reveals only their conceptual forms. It's a good place to start, but it's limited. To examine the *power* of an archetype, your type of direct perception is necessary. In other words, you have to meditate on the full existence of the archetype, beginning with the form as you understand it and then tracing this back to its quality, force, and purpose.

With modest modifications, the archetypes of the Tarot, which was designed for our culture, could speak as well to someone of another culture. That's because the essence of an archetype is more important than the form. In fact, this is why I was able to work comfortably with the I Ching, even though I wasn't Chinese. And of course, both the I Ching and the Tarot *are* widely used all over the world as tools for divination and teaching.

You're well aware of my interest in the unconscious. The use of the Tarot, which activates a system of archetypes, can teach virtually anybody about his own unconscious and the chambers within. For this reason, I suppose anybody who really wants to get to know himself can do so using a tool like this. Indeed, an individual's grasp of archetypal symbols is a very important key to developing the full use of the mind, because it links abstract and concrete thoughts. The Sabian card system [see glossary] that you use does the same thing with another set of archetypes. The lady who developed it has had some rather great insights into the operation of the unconscious.

Leichtman: Could one study the Egyptian or Greek pantheon of gods in somewhat the same way, with the realization that they are aspects of the forces of nature?

Jung: Yes. That's very well put. In fact, that kind of study would place one in touch with the origin of pure forces, that is, the Deva kingdom. [*Chuckling*] I was trying to make up an appropriate word, but someone over here told me to use the term "Deva kingdom." These *are* the forces of nature. They are not mere myths; they have an existence apart from human invention.

Leichtman: Yes. Let me ask something about a possible area of confusion in the study of archetypes. While thinking or meditating, is it possible to miss the actual archetype and run instead into a related thought-form prevalent in racial consciousness?

Jung: Well, Doctor, a thought-form prevalent in racial consciousness *is* an archetype, the way I defined it in my work. Knowing what I know now, however, I would call it a "meta-archetype." Many meta-archetypes exist in people's minds. Frequently that makes for a great deal of confusion.

Leichtman: I am thinking, for example, of the difference between the real presence of Jesus versus a fundamentalist Christian's *idea* of Jesus. You see?

Jung: Yes, I understand you. But even so, the sweet, Nordic image of Jesus that most people grow up with in Western civilization is a strong enough thought-form that it *is* almost an archetype. And the real Presence can work through that, when He chooses

[23]

to. That does not mean, however, that the thought-form will always entertain the real Presence. A meta-archetype can also be animated by what I will call ''small intelligences'' on the finer side of things— sometimes with rather drastic results. This is the real problem with meta-archetypes.

I realize now that you're referring to some writings of Mr. Leadbeater [C.W. Leadbeater, who will be interviewed in the next book in this series] about a budding psychic running into what amounted to a stage set complete with ''plaster of Paris'' figures which seemed to walk and move. This person thought she was receiving a clairvoyant vision of angels, when all she was actually getting was a thought-form of angels manipulated by a small intelligence. I don't want to label these small intelligences malicious or anything of that sort; they're really no more malicious than a cat or dog—they're just amoral. And they're quite playful. They don't seem to realize that there is any responsibility for animating these stage sets—the stage set being, of course, the meta-archetype, and the little intelligence being like a puppeteer.

Leichtman: Is it correct to say that these meta-archetypes have their existence on what we would call the astral plane?

Jung: Actually, much of what I called the collective unconscious has its existence on the astral plane, and meta-archetypes are part of that. This is where one could dip into all the thinking and feeling of mankind, mass consciousness. Some of it is unpleasant, but other aspects are important and useful. And this is where the little intelligences have their existence, too. For that matter, what you think of as the subconscious has most of its existence on the astral plane. There are parts of it elsewhere as well.

Much of the foolishness that comes out of seances and careless psychic work has its origin in all this. To go back to your point about the pink and Nordic Jesus, naive psychics will often clairvoyantly see a marionette or an animated dummy standing in a glowing light and spewing forth cliches. [*Laughter.*] But, of course, this is really something akin to a marionette show. All they've been doing is dipping into the meta-archetype department. For some types of people, this could be very reassuring and inspiring. When it is, okay. But most of the time it's really rather foolish. Can you imagine *anyone* doing important work in the world talking in circuitous sentences covered with ''frosting, nuts and raisins, and whipped cream''? Anyone who has the mentality to be a leader in any field is certainly going to proceed from point A to point B as directly as possible and without hesitation, ruffles, or flounces.

Leichtman: Yes. I want to ask you now about a different variety of archetype, if indeed it is an archetype. I'm referring to the concept of a ''personal myth,'' meaning the symbolic representation of a person's destiny. Is this a type of ''personalized archetype''? Does it contain the essence and power of one's personal destiny?

Jung: To argue that, one would have to assume that the immortal part of any being is an archetype. I would rather say no. The package of one's destiny and personal myth is really that aspect of the immortal being that is projected into the personality. In terms of events on the physical plane and an individual's awareness of them, the destiny may not be clear or meaningful to the personality. It is meaningful, however, to the entire being—the immortal part.

Leichtman: So, that package of the destiny and the personal myth would influence several incarnations, then?

Jung: Yes, yes. Incidentally, the idea of the immortal part of the human being is something I did know about. It was difficult to put that kind of idea into my writings, but any number of physical experiences made me aware of it. I remember all of the people I watched die in my lifetime; I realized that they were not really gone. There was something more to their lives than what I had been acquainted with. I especially remember two cases of my own relatives dying when I was sitting with them. A moment after the soul took flight, as they used to say, there was just such a complete, intimate feeling of being with that person. In each case, the feeling lasted for several minutes.

Leichtman: Yes. That sounds similar to what Stewart Edward White [who is interviewed in the last book in this series] experienced when his wife Betty passed on. He wrote about it in *Across the Unknown* and *The Unobstructed Universe*.

Jung: Yes. By the way, he and I have had some rather interesting discussions over here, and we both wish we could have met while in the physical. Of course, it was impossible.

Leichtman: There are many people, including many Jungian psychologists, who will read this account and automatically label our conversation as a dialogue with David's higher self.

Jung: Well now, you have talked about psychiatric

ideas with David, and you know how far over his head you usually go, don't you?

Leichtman: Yes.

Jung: If David were sitting here discussing these ideas, he would talk in terms he could understand. He is, I daresay, a good, practical psychologist, but he's not trained in psychology. He finds my writings fairly comfortable, but he's completely lost in the morass of language of other psychologists.

Maybe there ought to be a dictionary for lay people, so they can more easily read these writings. I notice that certain book clubs are selling to the general public highly technical treatises on the workings of the mind. A good dictionary is necessary, I'm afraid, because the general public is not sufficiently acquainted with the basics of psychology to understand what it's reading. There is a large language barrier that needs to be overcome.

Leichtman: Then how can we be sure that we're really talking to the actual "archetype" of Jung, rather than a mythical aspect of David's higher self? How does one stamp out doubt about this?

Jung [chuckling]: Well, of course, you are *not* talking to my archetype. You're talking to an extension of my being that was the intellect of Jung.

Leichtman: Yes, *I* know that. And I can say that you do not sound—that is, talk—like David. You sound like an aspect of Carl Jung speaking through David. But is there any other way that one could know for sure?

Jung: No, not really. Somewhere in the Bible it indicates that the things of the spirit have to be discerned by the spirit. I suppose any intelligent person speaking to a spirit through a medium will always have some doubts about the identity of the being he's entertaining—whether it's an apparition, a figment of the medium's subconscious, a ringer, just plain fraud, or the spirit the entity claims to be. Giving tests to obtain so-called evidential trivia, such as the maiden name of the spirit's grandmother or the name of the puppy dog the spirit had when he was a child, does not really produce the solid proof that some people assume it to be. Such finite ideas can, after all, be telepathically stolen by any clever spook or medium. I'm getting some assistance with these comments from some of my friends in spirit.

Knowing the identity of a spirit is not the real test of the value of a communication, however. The value is determined by the quality of what is said. The real test, therefore, is a line of enquiry that probes the nature of the being the medium is entertaining: his insights, experiences, compassion, and dedication to duty. Those are the true hallmarks of a person's humanity. By looking for them, any average, intelligent person sitting here—or reading the book—would soon have a sense that I actually do sound like the real Dr. Jung. Isn't that nice? [*Giggling.*]

You know, this type of evaluation applies not only to mediums, but also to the examination of any phenomenon. I certainly found it necessary in dealing with the collective unconscious. You can only go so far in studying anything on the basis of what large groups of people seem to experience in their dreams, myths, and habits. To go beyond this collective experience, which is always going to be tapped at a low common denominator, you must examine your own associations and reactions, hopefully at as deep a level as possible. This is where you can obtain real proof—your own realizations, where you are certain that this is the truth beyond all doubt. Unfortunately, this is not the type of experience or proof you can share scientifically. Talking and writing about such realizations reduces them to anecdotes.

One of the occult authors you like so well, Doctor, repeatedly warns readers that the material he has presented must not be accepted as dogma; rather, it must be tested by the careful thought and experience of the student. You have to use the same procedure for testing what comes through a medium—or, for that matter, through your own intuitive perceptions.

David, of course, usually knows when he plays back the tapes of these conversations that they contain valuable ideas he didn't know about before.

Leichtman: And he isn't dredging them out of his own personal unconscious?

Jung: No. There would be no source for much of this in his personal unconscious. As a matter of fact, he's not dipping into the collective unconscious, either, because some of this material would not even be there. At least it would not be readily obtainable. It certainly would not be organized in such a way that a medium could pick it up and focus it as a voice speaking through him.

You're familiar, I believe, with the book about the tape recordings of thousands and thousands of voices, all saying meaningless things. I'm reading David's memory of it, but it's rather sketchy. He only looked at the book briefly.

Leichtman: That must be *Breakthrough*.

Jung: Yes. They are not meaningless—

Leichtman: Fragmentary?

Jung: Well, they are about as meaningful as ordinary small talk.

Leichtman: I consider it ''thought static.''

Jung: No, it's not. These are actually the voices of departed beings who were doing the equivalent of making phone calls to one another. Those tape recordings tapped into what you call ''Father Bell,'' and were recording several conversations at the same time.

Leichtman: I was referring to the disjointedness and irrelevance of some of the comments. They had very little personal reference to those who tuned in to them. As you just said, it was like hearing an extra conversation on a phone call to a friend. You can hear it, but it has little relevance.

Jung: Well, there's another aspect of this to consider, too: on the other side of the veil, some people seem to continue the rather banal existence they led in the physical. They have the equivalent of tea parties and cocktail parties, complete with scenery. Many of these people have to go through things like that until it is time for them to come back to the physical plane.

Leichtman: To change the subject a bit, would you have any new insights into the process of ''giving birth to the Self,'' as you defined it in your work? I refer to the integration of unconscious content with physical consciousness.

Jung: That's a good question. It may be a bit difficult to answer, because some of the concepts involved don't translate well into language. The process of giving birth to the Self is enormously complicated. The entire being associates itself with the physical body as soon as the body is conceived. It doesn't necessarily live in the egg or fetus, but it does participate in the development of the body. Of course, the entire being can still operate on the other side of things somewhat independently. The integration of unconscious material into the physical personality also begins at about the same time, as strange as that might sound. I'm sure you know about people who, when under hypnosis, remember things that happened when they were a fetus, hearing everything that was said around them.

Again, this is something I could not have written about. So I want to take this opportunity to express some ideas on a new concept. There's something I want to label "the awake." The awake is that aspect of your entire being which picks up stimuli from the world—physical events, emotions, and all the rest. It is always functioning—in utero, in sleep, while anesthetized, in coma, and even in death. The awake's role is to collect this input and absorb it. The awake is *not* the subconscious, at least not the subconscious as you ordinarily think of it. It is the *entire being* that is always awake—the awake, as I am defining it, is the mechanism of wakefulness for the entire being, not just the subconscious. I want people to be aware of that distinction. There *is* a symbiotic relationship with the subconscious, of course. The subconscious begins to process and integrate what the awake has registered.

Leichtman: Do you have anything new to say about how one could consciously accelerate this integration during his adult life? In particular, I'm referring to healthy people who'd like to become more human. How can the average person who isn't considered sick achieve greater maturity?

Jung: Well, there needs to be greater communication and cooperation between the conscious and unconscious aspects of the personality. This would have to start with more awareness of the contents and operation of all dimensions of the mind. The careful examination of the mind—particularly the sources of one's thoughts and memories—would be necessary. In time, it would help acquaint one with the awake.

Leichtman: You mean looking for—

Jung: The process begins with what you call mental housecleaning. But it's more than that. Someone exploring the contents of his mind in a healthy and mature fashion would tend to find the ''skylight'' in his island. He would also probably find the ''secret entrance,'' if there is one. Not everyone has a secret entrance. He would be able to tap into more of the racial consciousness and archetypal levels of thinking as well.

Leichtman: Would this examination include looking for the extra meaning of events? The pursuit of the essence?

Jung: Yes. There's a growing trend in psychology to do just that—to look for meaning rather than illness or the roots of illness. As you have suspected, this search for meaning is one of the proper areas of investigation in parapsychology. It's going to have to be recognized as such. Again, I am pleased to confess that I am having something to do with promoting this idea.

Leichtman: Would you have any comments on the newer branches of psychology such as behaviorism, gestalt, the psychology of Ayn Rand and Nathaniel Brandon [objectivism], and so forth?

Jung: Without airing dirty linen, I am sorry to see

that there are several branches of contemporary psychology going back to treating infantile problems with infantile techniques. This just helps immaturity grow; it doesn't do anything to help the patient mature. Some of the contemporary work and experiments are going to produce important results, but not until they have been put into a different context.

One of these new branches advocates that people ought to express their affection by touching each other. Because of the growing impersonality of society, people do need to do this more often. And at times, it should also be included as a part of therapy. I refer to touching and relating in simple ways with strangers. People ought to know how to do this. But, I'm sorry to say, touching is often presented in a context that really doesn't do much good. It has almost become a party game. I'm sure some individuals are helped, but the conduct of these sessions is not terribly mature; it needs to be re-evaluated.

Going on with your question, I am very pleased with the branches of psychology that emphasize the evaluation of meaning. This is far more important than the classic approach of going after the roots of why you hate your mother, and so forth. It is much more healing to say: "So your mother was mean to you; but what is there about her that you can love?" Something of this sort would be a 180-degree switch from the classic approach, but that's just what is needed. Especially for those people who are more concerned with mental health than mental illness, the meanings are more important than the "why."

Incidentally, and I suppose that you know this, asking "why" is something of a trap; one can go around and around on a merry-go-round of "why." This idea has been paraphrased as: "Never ask God why; ask Him how." That really would be a more meaningful approach to one's own mental health.

Leichtman: Yes. I have often made the comment that certain varieties of psychological treatment seem to soothe the intellect and cure it of its problems, but the personality is still a mess, because it continues to hate and resent Mother—even though it understands why it does!

Jung: Yes, it's a mistake to endlessly talk about the hatred for Mother, because the very act of talking about it reinforces it. It would be much healthier to approach the whole situation from the standpoint of: "What do you love, and why do you love it, and can't you find something of that in Mother?" Of course, I am simplifying a very complicated process.

This type of therapy must be led by someone who is mature and compassionate. Unfortunately, as I look around the world, I find that many therapists and counselors are making no effort to become mature human beings. In many cases, they have lost sight of the compassion needed in their occupation.

Leichtman: Yes, indeed!

What about attempts to personify aspects of the subconscious and carry on a dialogue with it, either in meditation or through a competent therapist?

Jung: Certainly, this can be an excellent approach to self understanding. A competent therapist using that technique would do a great deal of good. Of course, it is a crutch to personify the subconscious— but a very effective crutch. The human mind tends to be animistic anyway. The subconscious loves to create personifications. It's often a good idea to take advantage of this. When one cannot walk without a crutch, the crutch needs to be there until the patient can put it away and walk without it.

This is one of the reasons I was so interested in the *I Ching*. I found it could be helpful when used by someone trying to find his own maturity. The human mind, being animistic, tends to put personalities on anything it sees. I can certainly vouch for the fact that the subconscious is very willing to associate itself with the *I Ching* and become it temporarily. I always appreciated the intelligence of the people who first thought out the *I Ching*, as well as the people who originally developed the Tarot, as there is a great deal of wisdom contained in them. So if the human mind has this kind of mechanism available to it, why not turn it into something that is constructive and maturing? That's one way of having a talk with a problem; i.e., by personifying it.

Leichtman: You are using, then, a set of symbols as a means of communicating directly with the contents of the subconscious and, indeed, the shadow.

Jung: Well, as you know, much of the content of the shadow is not in words anyway; that is, it doesn't translate into words.

Leichtman: Correct. Let me turn now to the events that surrounded the writing of your *Seven Sermons to the Dead*. Would you like to comment about why you wrote them?

Jung: I originally thought that was a teaching experience to help discarnate beings, but now I realize that it was really the reverse. The beings who crowded in on me in such numbers had come to teach me. They worked very much like Dr. Kammutt, whom you know. [Dr. Kammutt is an inner planes teacher who works with both Dr. Leichtman and Mr. Johnson.] They were quite tricky about the whole thing; they made me learn something by making it seem that they had something to learn from me. Of course, the relationship between incarnates and discarnates is really a two-way street. We learn from each other. But this was a very clever troop of spooks, if you will. They taught me something that I would not otherwise have made myself sit down and learn. I was rather pleased by that.

There were so many things I knew about, and wanted to pursue further, but was never able to get down in writing. Early in my career, for example, I was impressed with the vastness of the human mind and its capacity to know or do things without having to use any physical agency, even fingers. There was a musician whom I respected very much. The way he looked at the world, from his different perspective, gave me a great respect for the potential of the human mind. I tried most of my life to examine it from this standpoint of respect. Of course, when one is dealing with mentally ill people, one has a tendency to lose sight of that.

It is difficult to write coherently about how the mind works; to get anything across, you have to dissect the basic concepts. Suddenly, you're working with little pieces. I certainly never wanted to break any idea down in this way, but conventions have to be observed, I'm afraid. The problem is that too many people will take the pieces of a thought and use them out of context. They don't have the whole concept.

Leichtman: Yes, I share with you your concern about fragmenting the integrity of the human mind. This problem needs much more attention. Do you see a way in which psychology can evolve so that its concepts and methods derive from whole units of thought?

Jung: Several of my colleagues and I talked about this at a party once. We all realized that psychology would have to go in the direction of studying the mysteries of the human mind, and not remain stuck in working only with the tangible and observable behavior of patients. It will have to become far more concerned with the *noble* elements of humanity: genius, inspiration, creativity, compassion, personal honor, sacrifice, commitment, courage, and dignity. And eventually, it will have to include a serious and mature study of the occult and psychic phenomena. There is a beginning of that now, of course, in parapsychology. But parapsychology is falling short of its promise as a science, because it is hardly out of its diapers yet. Hopefully, it will mature in time.

I am very glad to see that psychologists are starting to appreciate the importance of the intangible components of the human mysteries. Their initial attempts to work with this have been elementary, of course: they have tried, for example, to measure and weigh the impact love has on another person. But eventually, this measuring and weighing will be done in a more realistic way—by taking a mental event and dealing with it in its own terms and on its own level. That will have to be—and it's also the direction that the study of parapsychology will have to go in. The endless collection of trivia and concrete measurements will not serve the needs of mankind. I know you and David have discussed this notion several times at length.

Leichtman: Yes. And, it's important to note that you set a good example in studying the archetypes *by their effects in a person's behavior!* You measured the quality and form of the archetypes by studying the response to them in individuals and groups. And the same will have to be done for psychic events and their effects.

I would like to go back for a moment and talk about the collective unconscious again. Could this be considered a sort of psychic sea that surrounds and influences everyone?

Jung: Yes, that's a very good analogy, because it really is a sea. Of course, I can see it now, although it's difficult for a physical person to see it. It's very much like a sea. It has tides. It also has pollution, and it has its native denizens as well. These denizens are not creatures of the human imagination; they exist apart from our minds. In a sense, they are ''fish'' that swim in this psychic sea; they are born in it, not in our minds. I don't mean that these denizens are literally fish; this is an analogy. They are the ''small intelligences'' I referred to earlier. They live in this sea of the collective unconscious. They are neither good nor bad. The book you like so much about the dwellers in the deep mind [*The Mind Parasites*, by Colin Wilson] describes some of these things.

There is a bit of a dichotomy here. One type of mind parasite is a creation of the human personality which has been repressed, taking on a life of its own to a degree. But another form of mind parasite is one of the denizens of the collective unconscious. I don't mean to make them sound malevolent, because they aren't. The fact that they feed on the substance of the ocean of the collective unconscious is no different than a fish feeding on the content of the water of the earth's oceans. It's just their natural environment.

Incidentally, the tides in the collective unconscious are also affected by the moon, just as the tides of the oceans of the earth are. This is why phenomena such as silly social behavior in large groups and mass murders happen at the time of a new or full moon. Fortunately, there's a positive side as well: at the time of the full moon, for example, the capacity to be influenced by archetypes is heightened.

You would be interested in this, Doctor—the whole universe, of course, has finer bodies. The astral plane includes astral versions of the planets and stars. And the astral and physical tides coincide, because the phases of the astral and the physical moons coincide. The point was well taken in *The Mind Parasites* that the moon has more of an effect on the collective unconscious than just the tides.

Leichtman: It seems to amplify or nourish these denizens of the astral.

Jung: Yes. You might call the moon of the astral plane one of those denizens, as a matter of fact, because the sea of the unconscious is rather deep—forty fathoms and then some! [*Laughter.*]

I'll have to tell you this: I had many clairvoyant experiences in my life. That should be obvious from what I left behind. My grasp of the collective unconscious came from a clairvoyant experience of seeing it. I don't think that this is particularly common, even among people who use their psychic ability day to day.

Leichtman: A friend and I were discussing, while

driving over here, the works of another popular psychologist, who writes about myths, madness, and mysticism. He tries to integrate all of these different types of human behavior in one framework. The point he makes is that it's all relative, depending on one's viewpoint. This is one of the current movements in psychology. What do you think of it?

Jung: Would you restate the last part of that? I missed something.

Leichtman: The question is: would you comment on psychologists who equate madness with mysticism, claiming that both are transcendent states?

Jung: Well, of course, that's rubbish. Madness is really a disconnection and disintegration in the physical and astral levels of personality. There's a notable lack of influence from the higher aspects of the entire being. Many times madness is a necessary part of an individual's life plan and has to be experienced, but that does not make it a transcendent state.

It is nonetheless true that a psychotic can occasionally have psychic experiences. After all, the moorings of his mind have already been loosened by the damage of his illness. The mystic, on the other hand, can have psychic experiences because he has *deliberately* loosened the moorings of his mind, using great self-control and intelligent planning. Now, I ask you: do those seem like similar states?

Leichtman: Good grief—of course not! The quality of the voices and visions perceived by a mystic is different than what a psychotic experiences.

Jung: Yes. There are some psychotics who do come up with amazingly accurate predictions. But the phenomenon doesn't last—it's very erratic. The work of a mystic, however, continues and grows.

Leichtman: And certainly a psychotic is unable to integrate his visions and psychic experiences with his personality.

Jung: The point is, if anyone is going to receive any benefit at all from a mystical experience, he has to be in control. There must be some sort of structure to it. And that, of course, is the antithesis of madness.

There are many, many people who cannot see the logic in mysticism because they have had a rather rigid, scientific background. The two sometimes don't seem to be compatible, but I was delighted to find that there are many similarities. It's a question of shifting gears in the mind. Unfortunately, very few people are willing to do that.

The current popularity of the occult and psychic phenomena exposes many people to the unconscious realms of life. Some of the people who get into these things are only interested in playing with them. If they have loose moorings to begin with, they can suffer some personality damage. That does not mean that studying the occult induces madness. It just means that certain people are psychotic to begin with, and they need to stay out of the occult because it won't help them.

Unfortunately, some people use the study of the occult as an excuse for irrational behavior. Sometimes going to a psychiatrist is used as an excuse for irrational behavior, too. That doesn't make psychiatry wrong, either.

Leichtman: My experience is that some people, when they go to a doctor, are only looking for a license to be sick.

[41]

Jung: Oh, yes.

Leichtman: Is it correct to say that archetypes, as you define them, represent a glimpse of the reality behind human behavior?

Jung: Yes. And if they were approached in the right way, they would even provide a glimpse of the reality behind that.

Leichtman: I find an intriguing parallel between your discussion of archetypes and the way the Kabalah is meant to be studied. They are both symbolic representations of vast *forces.* There could be no end to the series of realizations regarding them.

Jung: Oh, absolutely. Of course, I was limited to talking about psychology in my lifetime. I don't have those limits today, do I?

I know that interest in reincarnation is again popular in the world. Many people will ask, if they've lived before, why don't they remember it? Of course, a certain number of the archetypes of an individual, and the way they operate in that individual, *are* a type of memory—an unconscious memory.

There can't be an archetype without a meaning. In some cases, that meaning points very clearly to previous lives. I remember having a dream which profoundly affected me. In it, I found myself in the upper story of a house that I knew was mine. As I went downstairs, I discovered other stairs leading to even lower levels. The further I went, the more ancient the setting became. I was strongly impressed that these represented earlier levels of my own consciousness.

Leichtman: The occult term ''Dweller on the Threshold'' must be this collection of archetypes drawn from many past lives. Is that correct?

Jung: Yes, yes. The "Dweller on the Threshold" is something that, hopefully, one meets while going through analysis. I don't remember offhand if I ever got that idea put together.

Leichtman: Well, you certainly hinted at it in your concept of the shadow, didn't you?

Jung: Yes, but it's not the same as the shadow. The shadow is a boundary line, actually between several things, that takes on a personification.

I want to go back to some ideas we talked about a little earlier, because they are appropriate now. We were talking about the future of psychology and how it must probe the real depths of man's mind. And we were also discussing the idea of a psychology for healthy people, a psychology of maturity. The training one must take to be a mystic or an enlightened psychic would be a very good foundation for such a psychology. I tried to state this idea in my career, without being terribly obvious about it. Achieving mental health should almost be like the training an initiate would receive after entering a temple of the Ancient Wisdom. I hope that someone will be inspired to take up the skein of that thought.

I don't know if this is true or not—maybe Freud will tell you about it himself. But he told me on one occasion that it was his interest in mythology and the occult that gave his career its special direction. He began to realize that these traditions, because they have been in existence in the world so long, must contain some truth. So this gave him the impetus for his career.

Leichtman: I'm glad you mentioned that. More psychologists need to understand that the roots of psychology are mysticism and the occult. Until the science of psychology emerged, the only tools we had for self transformation were these traditions. It's good to see that some branches of modern psychology are open to the study of this body of wisdom.

Jung: Yes. In fact, I'm helping to promote that in the humanist element in psychology now. This is a direction I was trying to go in, but in a busy life one does have to leave a number of things undone. You know, there is an aspect of this work that is directed from the inner planes. That's part of the work I'm involved in.

Leichtman: I want to continue talking about the humanistic branch of psychology in a moment, but first I am eager to ask about the current preoccupation with psychological games. What is the correct perspective on this aspect of modern psychology? Some people think it explains all human behavior.

Jung: Well, even though many doctors are now defending games as a natural part of life, the idea of playing games is not going to lead to maturity at all.

Leichtman: Not even the playing of more sophisticated games?

Jung: No. It is still more sophisticated ''Monopoly.'' At least, that's my opinion. Mental health has to be approached by aiming for maturity, not by indulging one's childishness. Much of the trouble in society and the world today is due to the fact that many people approach life as if it were a game. They don't feel responsible for their actions; they think they just need to know a more convenient set of rules. Many people, unfortunately, are not well motivated: they want a pill for everything. That is what the games have become, too: the game player, by playing a game, avoids an understanding of himself. The only understanding that he gains is how to manipulate other people's mental problems so that he can effect a certain advantage. Now, I put it to you, Doctor: isn't that exactly what certain forms of witchcraft are?

Leichtman: Yes, I think that's right on. I, too, have noticed that people who become so interested in playing games and learning all about them seem to have some sort of devious intent in mind. They're interested in manipulating people rather than helping them.

Jung: Some of those people ought to stop playing their games long enough to look at their own minds; they would be shocked by what they found.

The work of mental health is not easy. Well, nothing worthwhile is easy, really. The modern trend to simplify things and capsulate them and make them pretty isn't doing any real good. The people who advocate that are making things too easy, and are devaluating their own minds by doing so.

Leichtman: In terms of what you've already mentioned, what would a proper humanistically-oriented psychology be like? How should it evolve?

Jung: Well, at this point in time, a humanistic type of psychology is the only hope of a healthy psychology. When psychology can enter the realm of the *real workings* of the human mind without fear or apologies, then we will have something worthwhile. The real workings, of course, include being psychic in the sense of psychic phenomena—being precognitive and clairvoyant.

Leichtman: You're absolutely right. Since consciousness actually exists in non-physical planes and deals with non-physical energies, I suppose psychic awareness is the only way to *directly* apprehend its operation.

Jung: In the field of parapsychology, the Russians have already gone back to the occult for a fresh approach. Some of this has been reported in a popular book [*Psychic Discoveries Behind the Iron Curtain*, by Sheila Ostrander and Lynn Schroeder]. But there are other developments that never got put into the book— and aren't likely to be shared with outsiders.

The Russians have made some great strides. They have gone back to the vast repositories of occult literature in Europe and Russia. America doesn't have these extensive resources. In fact, as psychology in this country becomes more aware of the value of occult knowledge, much of the research that will be needed will have to come out of Europe, because the literature is just not available in the United States.

If nothing else, there's one thing I grasped about the occult: most occult studies represent thousands of years of people looking at other people. I'm going to restate something that you said or were leading up to. Most psychologists get so involved in their theories and statistics that they never bother to look at their patients.

Leichtman: You mean the proper study of mankind really is man?

Jung: Yes, of course. The most valuable textbook in psychology comes with a leather binding, and the name on it is in gold. It is the patient. It is very true that an enlightened psychiatrist is taught by his patients.

Leichtman: Would it be helpful for psychologists to be able to examine their patients with intuitive skills as well as with traditional methods—that is, if they can develop them?

Jung: This is going to have to be done. Actually, there are, here and there, enlightened psychiatrists who are already doing this exact thing. How they do it, and how they acquire the ability to do it, is something that varies a great deal. Some of them have received formal instruction that helps them grasp it more readily. Others have just grown into it because their dedication to help their patients has invoked it. Their compassion is teaching them how to be intuitive. I know that, for myself, I did my best work when I could somehow almost merge with the patient. I am sure that this is a psychic phenomenon.

Leichtman: You're implying, then, that a psychologist could directly experience a patient's state of consciousness, rather than simply observe the effects of that patient's consciousness in what he does and says?

Jung: Yes. This is exactly what is going to have to happen. Of course, psychologists will throw up their hands in horror at this idea. Yet, if they would think of themselves as teachers rather than healers, perhaps they'd be more effective. Many dedicated teachers are able to work intuitively, which helps them better understand their students.

Leichtman: Are you saying, then, that true healing occurs *within* the patient or person: a therapist can work most effectively by teaching the patient to heal himself?

Jung: Yes. But that concept should not be limited to illness. Psychology should teach healthy people how to progress toward maturity. I notice in the world now that the idea of maturity frightens a lot of people—they confuse it with growing old. And they are afraid of growing old. Yet this is unwarranted—it can be a beautiful stage of life. One can develop a bond of oneness with the entire world, and this produces a marvelous sense of security. One's fears are not that important anymore, because there's not that much to fear. This sense of oneness and security is what both of these states, old age and maturity, are about. Now, I ask you, Doctor—is that anything to be frightened by?

Leichtman: Of course not. And I like the way you describe maturity. Can you say a little more about its nature, though? As you know, some people define maturity as the absence of neurotic traits. I take it that you think of maturity as a presence of wisdom, compassion, courage, and competence.

Jung: Yes, these are the elements of maturity. And it's important to realize that there are traces of these elements in everyone. Psychologists should respect these noble elements in their patients, instead of being obsessed by disease. That's the first step toward helping someone develop his maturity.

Having said that, I think it's valuable to add that a certain amount of what seems to be neurotic thinking is necessary. It adds color to life. It adds color to experience. Some of these little ''neurotic'' tendencies are not so terrible. I daresay they can even be a part of maturity. I'm *not* saying that you have to be neurotic to be mature. That's a contradiction of terms. I know you have said this, Doctor, but it was my idea first: geniuses are geniuses *because* of their ''neurotic traits," not *in spite of* them. Far from being flaws in their personality, these little traits are vital parts of the temperament that gives them their genius. The Bohemian characteristics of an artist, for example, must be respected as a part of the fabric of his genius, not scorned as neurotic rebelliousness. Any genius, therefore, will have some trouble adjusting to society and his own uniqueness, but it's wrong to consider this difficulty a neurosis.

Leichtman: Of course, not everyone who appears to be neurotic is a genius; he may just be sick.

[*Laughter.*]

Jung: Yes, of course.

Leichtman: I say that for those who might be looking for a license to be sick.

Jung: Well, automobiles have wheels and so do roller skates; that doesn't make them the same.

[*Laughter.*]

Leichtman: Speaking of wheels, I think it's time to move on to a different subject. [*Groaning.*] How do you like my free association? [*Hissing and booing.*] Well, that's what I wanted to ask you about—free association. [*Laughter.*]

The use of free association is a well-established technique in psychoanalysis. But now some people are advocating the use of symbols or images in free association, rather than ideas or memories. Is this a helpful advancement for psychoanalysis?

Jung: No, it's just an expansion of something that's already been going on.

The association mechanism of the human mind is so important to the richness of thinking that it deserves to be studied in its own right. Think about this for a minute. The reason why mankind has enjoyed art—the art of painting, the art of sculpture, and the art of architecture—is because art stimulates rich associations in the mind of each viewer. Great artists are great because they've learned how to manipulate these associations. So you see, the associative capacity of the mind can be quite enriching. Certainly it's a very handy tool for a psychiatrist to use to help patients.

Leichtman: I suppose it's about the only way of going fishing in your personal unconscious, or at least in the shadow.

Jung: Oh, yes. This is another reason, incidentally, why I was very interested in things such as the Tarot and the *I Ching*. They were so "imagy," if I can say it that way. That's one of David's words, but I like it. Even images in the Bible were meant to be liberally used in free association. Frankly, I wrote many of my books and articles leaving only some dots and clues. I hoped that readers would associate with these clues and then go on from there in their own minds. This is, after all, one of the approaches to creativity.

Leichtman: Can one free associate with feelings as well as with symbols, images, and memories?

Jung: Sure, because associations are chains of many, many things. Some of them may seem to be unrelated. In trying to get a picture of the inner workings and inner landscape of a patient's mind, an analyst should realize that any image can be connected with an emotion, a state of mind, a remembrance of something that happened at the age of five, a remembrance of Mother's smile, a remembrance of a sister's doll, and on and on. Tracing the connections of these associations can provide the analyst with a roadmap of the patient's consciousness, if he is astute. This is also something that people can do for themselves quite easily.

Leichtman: In fact, that's the way I like to think of your writings—as providing a roadmap of human nature.

Jung: It's very kind of you to say so. I had hoped that my work could serve that kind of purpose and perhaps inspire readers to expand their own associative roadmaps. Reading really should be enjoyable work. Too many people want to read what is there but do not want to do the work of understanding what is there.

Leichtman: Yes, I suppose reading should be an act of communing with your own higher self or spirit. Certainly your own higher self should be reading along with you.

Jung: Yes, of course. One can also engage his own animistic ability and make the book a living thing with which to commune.

Leichtman: Yes. I believe a very fine analyst and admirer of your work, Dr. Ira Progoff, recommends that you read a book, put it aside, and then develop a dialogue with it.

Jung: Yes, that's a very fine technique. As a matter of fact, I used that later on in my career, as a means of working out problems with patients. I would see them for their appointment, and then, later on, I would have a purely mental dialogue with their essence. It helped me to find ways of assisting them better.

Leichtman: Do you think you were actually in touch with their essence, or were you only reviewing your memories of the earlier session?

Jung: Oh, no—I was aware at the time that I was contacting their essence.

Leichtman: I suppose there are some who would doubt that, but I imagine these mental dialogues yielded some very useful results. One could evaluate the worthiness of that technique on that basis.

Jung: Well, I don't know how Dr. Progoff does this, but I developed my technique by trial and error. I had a number of mental dialogues in which I dealt with what was going wrong with the patient. Then I discovered that if I had a mental dialogue with the healthy part of that same person, I could more clearly understand the nature of the problem and how to lead that person to health.

Leichtman: You were talking, then, with the healing essence of that patient.

Jung: Well, I would call it the pattern of the patient. I think anyone's pattern is healthy.

I'm going to let David up now.

Leichtman: One last question. Would you be willing to have a bit of a dialogue with Dr. Freud, if he is available and if Paul is willing?

Jung: Oh, yes. Dr. Freud would be delighted.

[*After a break for dinner, the interview was resumed, with Dr. Sigmund Freud appearing through Paul Winters, and Dr. Jung continuing to appear through Dave Johnson.*]

Jung: Where is it that we can pick up the pieces?

Leichtman: One of the last things we were talking about was the contribution psychic psychiatrists could make to the development of a psychology of health.

Jung: Well, I suppose we ought to add some

comments about the outward signs of health, such as laughter and self-acceptance. It's probably safe to assume that the person who goes about his work softly smiling and humming is a mentally healthy person, a person poised in the universe. That's the nature of the problem, you know—our poise in the universe.

Freud: That is not to say that one should go around humming to be healthy.

Leichtman: Or giggling? [*Laughter.*]

Jung: Oh, no—that's not what I meant. It's an outward sign of mental happiness and maturity, not necessarily a means of obtaining it.

Freud: I must interject here that being the brunt of sexual jokes has been some joy to me, at least in the past few years, because the joking is done in a spirit of self-acceptance, and that's healthy. However, the doctors themselves, especially the psychiatrists who are following my work, have somewhat overdone the sexual overtones. While sexuality was an important part of my work, I'm afraid my theories about it have been somewhat misused.

Jung: Well, young people must realize that in our era, sex was far more repressed than it has ever been during recent times. It was a taboo topic of conversation. As such, in our time it was one of the major sources of mental illness or psychic disease.

Freud: Yes. That was a particular era when the sexual mores were repressed in mass consciousness, as you call it. It was necessary to go out on a limb to bring all of this out. That was part of the work I tried to do. We are now seeing a tipping of the scales to the opposite extreme. There has been an overcompensation, which is necessary in the course of evolution.

[53]

At the risk of repeating myself, I would add that my concentration on the sexual aspect of the human being was necessary—looking at it in retrospect—because of the values of that time. And the success of my work helped set the climate for your discussion at dinner [some rather ribald joking about sexual material in popular magazines]. It's a healthy sign indeed that this can be expressed openly and humorously.

I have a few comments which we've discussed previously, Doctor, but I would like to bring them up for the purposes of this project. The work that I undertook necessitated the concentration of my personality on one particular subject. This overcompensation was necessary to bring out the inspiration to do my work.

Leichtman: Yes. I would look at it as an aspect of the specialization of the personality.

Freud: I suppose I might have been called neurotic; at least I was called neurotic in my last incarnation. And this may be somewhat true, but it was a necessity in order to concentrate on the subject.

Leichtman: Is it true, as I surmise, that the group of people who gathered around you in Vienna had all incarnated for the purpose of developing the science of psychology? And was it intended that you all specialize in one particular branch of psychology? Is that not true?

Freud: Yes, this is very true.

Leichtman: And indeed, wasn't this responsible for the apparent division of opinion and effort after a certain phase—so you all could go off and develop your particular specialties?

Freud: Yes. The seed was developed in the group we started in Vienna. We would hash over and discuss the human mind and psychology. I might add that we would do so rather violently at times.

Jung: I even remember several occasions of great book throwing fights. [*Several gasps.*]

Freud: Yes.

Leichtman: Ah hah! [*Laughter.*]

Jung: Books and other things.

Freud: It made quite a scene—psychologists throwing psychological terms at one another.

Jung: And books as well!

Freud [*laughing*]: Yes.

Jung: I mean literal books; it didn't matter what the subject was, as long as it was a handy missile. Our battles were akin to the throes a group of artists goes through when it is trying to hash out a theory of art that would be acceptable to everyone in the group. Of course, none of them is going to find *a* theory of art that is acceptable to *all* of them. They are entitled to their own opinions. And this was very true of us because, as I look at it now, psychology is really more of an art than a science. And that is the way it always will have to be, because we aren't dealing with something that will always happen the same way.

Leichtman: I suppose it is because each individual is different, and his problems will have to be approached creatively and uniquely.

Freud: Yes, and this is a problem in psychology today. A literal reading, word for word, of the psychological theories that we set down cannot be applied to every individual. There should be as many specific psychological theories as there are individuals. I would hope that the ideas that the two of us put forth would be added to by others.

Our ideas are distinctly dissimilar, as you know, although their roots intertwined in our original talks. They are two persons' distinct interpretations of the human mind, and I would hope that they would be considered as that, and not as the law. They are something to work from and build upon.

Jung: A law in our field is something that is not really possible. A physicist can dogmatically state a law about the behavior of physical objects. A psychologist dare not be that dogmatic, because the behavior of human personalities is not always predictable. With all honesty, I don't think that there can be *a* law that governs human reactions. To be sure, there are principles that govern behavior, but their application to each individual is unique. I'll say it this way, and I mean this with a scientific purpose: God in His great wisdom made us individuals.

Even one individual will change and transmute. I remember recognizing this several times in patients. I would be going along with a person, and suddenly there would be a vast change. It wasn't a change of direction, and it wasn't that I had been giving the wrong therapy or that he had been lying to me. It was just that suddenly, he was different that particular day. The only way he could explain it was that his body chemistry had changed for some reason. It was very difficult to keep on top of these changes all the time. I know we both made mistakes; every psychiatrist in the world makes mistakes, because it is so difficult—even in dealing with one person—to be on top of the tides of that person's psyche at all times.

Freud: Very well put. I might interject that it's quite a thrill to be part of this project, sitting next to an old colleague of mine—even though we had our differences.

Jung: I must confess that I remember our days in Vienna. The good Doctor here would not teach. He would allow us to have a conversation—the whole mess of us. [*Snickering.*] I suppose that we were like puppies or something of that ilk. He would let us go on and on, and then he would say: "I would like to interject one thought." And *he* would then go on for two hours. [*Laughter.*] I appreciate now that this is a rather masterful way of teaching.

Freud: Yes. I would like to add that the thought that a psychologist or psychiatrist ought to be a teacher is very well put. We, as a group in Vienna, were really psychiatrists to one another. We counseled each other and argued with each other.

Jung [*whispering*]: And drank with each other.

Freud [*chuckling*]: And threw books at each other. [*Laughter.*] And out of it came the birth of something very wonderful.

Jung: Well, we hope it's wonderful. The results aren't all in yet.

Freud: Well, we can keep tabulating them as we go.

Jung: I've been trying to describe the project that you and I are engaged in at the moment. Would you like to make some comments about that?

Freud: Well, the psychic aspect of the human mind is one that we both were aware of in our own little ways—especially later on in our careers.

Jung: I think we had better say "parapsychic" at this point.

Freud: Very good. Although it may not be that apparent in the usual interpretation of my writings, my

[57]

thoughts did change quite a lot as I progressed. This is true of anyone who explores the human mind. The background I came from gave me a deeper awareness of the finer aspects of the human mind—the parapsychic, as you might call it.

Jung: Thank you.

Freud: You're welcome. I want everyone to know that I did change a lot of my ideas during my career. Some people thought I changed too many of them. There were others, though, who didn't think I changed at all. [*Chuckling*] I believe one of them was you, Doctor. As I recall, you rather vigorously tossed about the notion that the only thing that kept me respected in psychology toward my later years was my name.

[*Laughter.*]

Jung: Well, you did effect some cures and improvements in a number of people, and this was something that was quite well known about you, too, you know.

Freud: Yes.

Jung: I suppose that is what keeps all of our noses clean. [*Laughter.*] Well, you know, it says in the Bible, "By their acts ye shall know them." What better way is there to promote a theory than to prove it by helping people?

Freud: Yes. The development of the basic elements of my theory was prompted by one of the great problems of my era—the repression of sexuality. I was also a bit repressed myself, and I was well aware of it. I would hope that my theories would be looked at in that perspective. There seem to separate groups of Freudians and Jungians—

Jung: Yecchh! [*Laughter.*]

Freud [*chuckling*]: You have such a way with words. [*More laughter.*] I hope that there will be a merging of the different approaches to the human personality. The workable and usable aspects of different schools of thought need to be brought together. Where something seems unreasonable, then other and more up-to-date ideas should be used in its place.

I believe I've eluded your question, Carl.

Jung: Standard operating procedure, as I recall. [*Giggling.*]

Freud: We are involved in a number of activities. On the inner planes, one does get a much different perspective of his work—that is, the work one performed while in the physical plane. Although one can intuitively grasp much of this while incarnate, it becomes much more apparent when one passes over and takes a look at his life and the work that was done. We both would hope that the parapsychic aspect of the mind will be looked at with an open mind by the psychologists of today. The old concepts that were set down should be used as a basis to go further into the wonderful mind of the human being.

Jung: Excuse me.

Freud: Yes?

Jung: My major criticism of modern psychiatry is the fact that modern psychiatrists, as a body, do not approach their work with an open mind. While I realize that we were the avant-garde of psychiatry—

Freud: There is even a poster of me! [*Laughter.*]

Jung: Oh, I see.

Leichtman: We forgot to bring it down, sir.

Freud: That's all right.

Jung: Of course, I shall be jealous. [*Laughter.*]

[59]

They are going to make sweat shirts after me. [*More laughter.*]

Freud: And Jungian tennis shoes? [*Laughter.*]

Jung: Jungian tennis shoes are designed to massage the libido by way of the feet.

Leichtman: Well, there are Freudian golf balls, aren't there? [*Laughter.*]

Freud: And Freudian candles.

Jung: And Jungian mandalas.

No, this is a very bad thing going on in the practice of psychiatry. I don't mean to damn any one—don't take it in that sense—but most psychiatrists and psychologists are not being compassionate enough. I talked about this earlier. They are not ''reading'' their patients. And most of them are not going into their work with an open mind.

Freud: No—they are *scientists!*

Jung: They are scientists. One, two, three, four—dot, dot, dot, dot! It's like when I did the waltz. One, two, three, four, skip—or something like that. I never did get it through my head. I remember crushing one poor lady's feet one evening, when I was very much trying to be dashing. I was in my fifties at that point. But this is what modern psychiatrists are doing; they are crushing their patients' feelings under foot.

Freud: They are crushing them with theories. They mold them and classify them.

Jung: Shape them, pack them, and sculpt them.

Freud: And shape them to fit the theory, rather than fitting the treatment to match the patient. Am I getting through? Or should I elaborate more?

Leichtman: Oh, I think you're quite right. You're

suggesting that psychiatrists take a flexible and practical approach to therapy in all cases.

Freud: Individualistic and humanistic.

Jung: I am going to interject a story. Late in my career, I found the leisure time to do much of my thinking about symbols. I had an occasion to meet one afternoon with another man. Dr. Freud was there as well—as a spirit.

Freud: We spooks can do that kind of thing, you know.

Jung: It was a very enlightening afternoon; we learned a great deal from the man about symbols and their structure. This man is still living in the physical plane: it's Salvador Dali [a surrealist painter] I'm talking about. He's very, very knowledgeable about symbols. You know, if you are going to explore the nature and function of symbols in an enlightened way, the most intelligent thing to do is to seek out a great artist and let him teach you.

Freud: Absolutely!

Jung: Dali, by the way, has a very fine, intelligent mind. He likes to talk of himself as a paranoiac. I found that he was anything but. I listened more than I talked, and it was a very interesting afternoon.

Freud: Yes, and one of the things I find rather distressing in this regard is the treatment some of the geniuses of today receive. This is a problem I ran up against in my lifetime as Sigmund Freud. The geniuses of today are often not treated as such; they are thought of as quacks, cranks—

Jung: Weirdos! Which is not to say that one has to appear to be a hippie to be a genius.

Freud: Yes, yes. But along with genius also goes a

wonderful, different, out-of-the-norm personality that in its own right should be studied. And instead, it is deemed by mass consciousness to be a deviation.

Jung [*whispering*]: And suspect!

Freud: And suspect, yes. I am afraid to say that genius is being dealt with in some rather inhumane ways. We would hope that people with genius would be accepted as a part of society wherever they are found. I might add that Thomas Jefferson was referring to this same idea when he discussed the freedom to be an American. [The interview with Jefferson is the seventh in this series.] This goes as well for the European countries and the rest of the world, for that matter.

Jung: I would even restate it somewhat, if you will forgive me, as the freedom to be human.

Freud: Very good.

Jung: And there is something else we need to consider. We are talking a great deal today about where psychology is heading, and we must also talk about where mankind is heading. Mankind must go toward being more human—more noble, poised, and talented. *This absolutely has to happen!*

Freud: And the first requisite is to accept *every* human being as an integral part of humanity, and to relate to one another in that spirit.

Leichtman: Do you mean even the psychotics and schizophrenics, the hallucinators and the madmen of the world?

Freud: Well, no one's totally mad. There are always inner, unconscious elements of sanity. Yes, these people, too, must be dealt with as a part of humanity and humanely treated. The practice of shutting people up in institutions is in itself very inhumane. Humanity must learn to take care of such people by helping them, instead of just throwing them away.

Jung: I noticed in my work that by listening to what we used to call a madman, I sometimes got a fresh look at the world, because the madman was looking at it *upside down.* I think, and I am going to say this in hyperbole, that if the gods had not made a few madmen, there would not have been either one of us!

Freud: That is very true, and I rejoice.

Jung: Yes. We are not rejoicing in someone's madness and misery; we are rejoicing in the fact that the world, through madness, has come to realize that madness is an important human condition that needs to be understood. And Dr. Freud is being very modest. We lived in a time when human sexuality was very much abused, misunderstood, and the subject of superstition. Dr. Freud gave most of his attention to sexual repression because, at that time, it was something that was driving society insane. He made great, great strides in understanding and in helping other people to understand the convolutions of their sexuality.

The part of his work that is most often overlooked is something which is discussed a great amount in this series of interviews. Were it not for sexuality, there would be no creativity. There would be no genius or free thinkers. There would be no great men of stature in history. There would be no mediums or psychics. All of these achievements are interrelated with one's sexuality. Since Dr. Freud has done his work—and I will blow his horn for him because he always was a very modest person—

Freud: Rooty-toot-toot! [*Laughter.*]

Jung: Ha! He gave modern man an understanding about his sexuality. Not everyone understands this yet. You know, there are still people who resent the science of psychiatry, because they think they will have to go to a doctor and talk about their sex life. In the last ten years on the physical plane, sex has at least become a civilized topic of conversation. Men and women at a party can engage in a disucssion about sex without that being a prelude to an affair, and without any embarrassment to anyone. Society, perhaps, is beginning to rid itself of a great sickness, of people considering a part of themselves to be nasty—a part that they don't want to face. Anything that society handles that way needs to be examined, because this is a sign of sickness in society. I'm sorry to see some circles of society treating psychic phenomena in exactly the same way now. The taboos in society are the first thermometer reading of a high fever. It should be a signal that there needs to be an examination of the disease and then an immunization.

Freud: The act of isolating anything such as sexuality by making it taboo is repressive. It packs away a wonderful part of our humanity and treats it as a disease, when it should be dealt with compassionately.

Jung [*puffing on a cigaret through David's mouth*]: This thing is not a cigar, but it will have to do.

Leichtman: I'll smoke one for Dr. Freud later. [Paul does not smoke.] Is there anything more you want to tell us about what you are doing on the inner planes?

Freud: Both of us have taken an interest in humanistically-oriented psychology. We hope that other

[64]

psychologists and psychiatrists will use what they have been trained in and add to that new interests, as we have.

Jung: And there are those that we hope will take what they have and throw it in the garbage can and take up steam fitting. [*Laughter.*]

Leichtman: Are you talking about the screamers and wailers?

Jung: I'm not going to label any of them. Anyone who has eyes to see will know what I'm talking about. We don't have to belabor the obvious.

Freud: If you'll just consider the word ''human,'' you'll know whom we're speaking about.

Jung: I can think of one modern branch of psychiatry that would really be more appropriately applied to primates than to humans. I don't even think that it would help the primates get well. [*Laughter.*] Primates could handle their problems quite well without benefit of doctors. They have done it, lo, these many millions of years.

Freud: I seriously doubt that they have problems with sexual repression. [*Guffawing.*] We are also working with what I suppose you might call occult psychologists.

Jung [*in tones of mock horror*]: Oh! Dare we say that? [*Laughter.*]

Freud: Yes, yes. Well, I think it's time. This is where psychology *must* go. Otherwise, there will be a whole new, natural field of knowledge coming up, and it will leave the psychologists behind. We certainly hope this will not be the case.

Leichtman: I believe something similar to that has occurred in the area of religion. Organized religion had the opportunity to absorb psychic phenomena, mediumship, healing, and even aspects of psychology, but for the most part it failed to do so. This has meant that these branches of human endeavor are estranged from their spiritual roots. As a result, both religion and these endeavors suffer.

Jung: Well said, Doctor. But do you suppose we could maybe get lucky and ''estrange'' a few parapsychologists here and there? [*Laughter.*] I think they're already strange.

Freud: Yes, if we can just give them some more machines...

Jung: I'm very happy to see that parapsychology is now accepted as a science. But without wishing to seem egotistical, I believe—in light of what I have observed and what I was able to do in my lifetime—I was light-years ahead of the current parapsychologists.

Freud: Absolutely!

Jung: Well, you were, too, of course, but you never published any of those things. I will have to tell a naughty story at this point. One afternoon, Dr. Freud did a card reading for me which was very enlightening. He was quite good at it.

Leichtman [*gasping*]: A card reading?

Jung: A card reading!

Leichtman: The gypsy in Freud revealed at last! [*Snickering.*]

Freud: My family was quite psychic, and this did stimulate some of these leanings, although I had other work to do. I was kept quite up to date with the latest developments. As a youngster, I learned a great deal about the parapsychic part of the human mind and how to use it, although I kept this fact hidden ''under my pillow.'' I suppose I can use that expression.

Jung: In English, it would be better to say ''hiding the light under your bushel.'' You see, in Viennese the expression would work out ''hidden under the pillow.''

Freud: Dr. Jung and I had quite a few discussions about the psychic aspect of the human mind, spooks, and so forth. I believe that even the ''spook complex'' was discussed at one time.

Leichtman: Yes. I believe that you, Dr. Freud, wrote Dr. Jung a letter expressing the hope that he would get over his ''spook complex'' one day. This was after the experience that led to the writing of *The Seven Sermons to the Dead.*

Freud: This was when I thought that he had gone off the deep end. [*Laughter.*]

Jung: Well, in spite of that, an interest in psychics is something we had in common, Doctor. I made an effort to interview many types of psychics in my city. I don't think this was terribly well documented—because I took pains to see that it wasn't.

Freud: Which was necessary at the time.

Jung: Yes. And there were occasions when I felt, particularly in some kinds of emotional situations—not emotional problems, but emotional situations—that it was better for me to refer one of my patients to a psychic.

I think that you said at one time, Doctor, that it sometimes is best to send a bereaved family to a good medium, so that they will understand that their relative is still alive and well. Enlightened psychiatry is going to be moving more and more in that direction. The vocal minority of parapsychologists are going to make

[67]

fools of themselves, but the quiet majority of psychologists are going to do *anything* to help their patients become better people, including investigating the psychics in the area—or reading dangerous and forbidden books about astrology and things of that sort.

Freud: I might just change the subject a bit. I noticed throughout my work the effect of thought, especially sexual thought, on certain patients. I was particularly interested in the impact of malevolent energy. I suppose you would call it psychic attack, Doctor. One of the first things I checked when I suspected that, and again this is not well documented, is the nature of the relationships the patient had with immediate personal contacts. I looked specifically for evidence of parapsychic elements in these relationships, and discovered that they were quite apparent— especially when there was a sexual problem. Even at a distance, thoughts could have a marked effect on a patient. It proved beneficial to bring in the people involved and discuss with them—rather discreetly, I might add—the occult impact of their thoughts on each other. This was part of the therapy.

Leichtman: You are talking about the purely telepathic transference of thoughts, aren't you?

Freud: Yes. It was very necessary to have them realize what they were doing to each other mentally. Even though this problem is readily apparent, the whole ramifications have not been examined or understood.

Leichtman: Would you go so far as to say that the problem of psychic attack is frequently associated with mental-emotional problems today?

Freud: Yes. If I may put it in these terms, the

whole of humanity has become somewhat more sensitive. Thus, the emanations coming from the power of each person have much more of an effect on others. This is a phenomenon that is increasing each day. And in the case of a person examining his own thoughts, he might find, after some introspection, that certain people stimulate specific types of thought in his own mind. These thoughts are quite distinct when he is with these people, and less so when he is not. This phenomenon was very apparent to me in reference to sexual interests, and I tried to deal with this in my patients as well as with some groups and even families. Is there anything that you can add to that, Carl?

Jung: I don't know if I can. I found that the symbiotic relationships between members of the same family were sometimes vampiristic to the point of absolute disgust. Unfortunately, the predatory aspect in some families is now getting much worse with the current rise of interest in the occult.

Freud: Yes. That is not discussed enough.

Jung: And some people that I would call ''amateur psychiatrists''—people who have read *a* book and then practice ''psychiatry'' on their families—are really practicing a form of vampirism which is quite deadly and withering to the people in the family.

Freud: I want to finish a few remarks here. One can review his own thoughts and feelings with the object of analyzing the changing qualities of them. This kind of review would help demonstrate the effects that other people have on one's thinking and attitudes. This telepathic effect is, of course, most obvious in the likes and dislikes people have for each other on first meeting. They get along with some people quite well;

others, they don't.

But when it comes to psychic attack, it can be a very vicious phenomenon. Certain people take it upon themselves to actually put mental needles into another person, mentally strangle another person, mentally visualize harm, mentally verbalize harm—

Jung: Excuse me. Even blighting everyone around them just by their own depraved mental state.

Freud: Yes. And one of the things that every person should do is take a look at how his thoughts change as he interacts with various friends, neighbors, relatives, and business associates. He should also evaluate his thoughts and feelings when he's alone, and note the difference in quality. If any reader of this book would just take time to do this simple experiment, he would make some startling realizations about which people affect his thoughts and how. Not so much how, but how the phenomenon is manifesting.

Jung: Or maybe even why!

Freud: Yes. I was led to this by the sexual aspect; that is, the sexual fear and sexual desires that one person would send telepathically to another, and the effect they would have. On many occasions, these sexual forces took the form of erotic fantasies that did not start until the patient had formed some new relationship, be it sexual or merely an acquaintance. These thoughts were remarkably different from the patient's ordinary thoughts and feelings. After a series of these experiences, it was quite apparent that these fantasies had been caused by an *external influence*, and had to be dealt with accordingly.

Jung: Do you suppose that modern psychologists would call that an "exfluence"? [*Laughter.*]

[70]

Leichtman: Was the content and quality of the patients' dreams also affected?

Freud: Yes, very much so.

Jung: I also observed that the content and quality of these erotic fantasies tended to create a kind of artificial guilt in my patients. It was a guilt that was not born of a thought that *they* had; it was *someone else's* thought and sometimes *someone else's* guilt.

Freud: Well, this went along with the times when sexual and erotic fantasies were met with loads of guilt. The mores of the day were quite explicit. The whole definition of humanity was asexual, and if anyone had sexual fantasies, he immediately considered himself an outcast, sick—

Jung: Cursed!

Freud: Yes. This was part of what I had to deal with. I might add that the telepathic effect of other people on my patients was more damaging than most people suspect, even today.

Leichtman: I presume that this impingement on the patient's stream of consciousness would also have an effect on his free associations while in therapy. This coloration might mislead the therapist, might it not?

Jung: A rather interesting phenomenon occurs with this sort of thing. There is a marked jolt in the stream of associations. When you are aware of this and are looking for an implant on someone else's thought in your patient's mind, the associations can be most revealing. They go along in recognizable patterns, but then suddenly, there is a jolt or shift. Suddenly, we are off on a pattern that is rather obviously not like anything else that has come out so far.

I might add this idea, too. We have been using the

word "psychic" in two different ways—to talk about the energies of the psyche and also to talk about parapsychic phenomena. The phrase "psychic attack" that we've been using would include both of these meanings of "psychic." Not only can someone blight and kill another person's psychic ability and psychic awareness through this kind of attack, but one can also kill the *structure* of the other person's personality. These attacks are both psychic and parapsychic.

Leichtman: I would hope that readers who have heard reports of plants being stunted or killed by being hated would comprehend that the human organism is equally or more sensitive to such negative feelings and thoughts, when they are directed at it. There is a rather famous novel written by an English occultist, Dion Fortune—*The Secrets of Dr. Taverner*. It has to do with an accomplished occultist treating victims of psychic attack and diseases of the occult. Do you foresee such a specialist actually being needed?

Jung: Well, Madame Violet—Dion Fortune to you [Dion Fortune was the pen name of Violet Firth]— was an accomplished psychologist as well as an occultist and writer. She was able to blend both the knowledge of the human mind and occultism quite well. She should be more of a model for psychiatric therapy than she is at the moment.

Freud: Yes. The occult methods of treating psychic attacks shouldn't be a separate field by itself. It should be incorporated into psychiatry and psychology, rather than having the local white witch come in and cast off negative energy.

Jung: In Europe, clinics of the type of Dr. Taverner are more common than you may suppose. In her own way, Dion Fortune was a pathfinder, too. She took training as a psychologist and then worked in these clinics.

Leichtman: I believe that one of the biographers of you gentlemen, Dr. Nandor Fodor, was able to combine his knowledge of occultism with the practice of psychology. He wrote a very good book called *Freud, Jung, and Occultism.*

Jung: He even worried me about *his* spook complex. [*Laughter.*]

Freud: That is quite a book, by the way. It puts a light on both Dr. Jung and me that is quite different and relevant to our work.

Jung: May I digress for just a moment? I would like to make a closing statement for myself and then turn over the rest of the evening to Dr. Freud, if you like and if he is willing.

Freud: Well, I don't have that much more to add.

Jung: I realize that I have left an idea unfinished. We were talking about games earlier. I would like to say, as a rule of thumb, that people who manipulate other people are doing it because they do not have the courage to face their own interior landscape. So they must manipulate other people into a game where they can put them down. And they do it in such a way that the victims end up feeling more guilty than the manipulators do. The games of life tend to be played by people who are manipulators, of one degree or another. Sometimes the ''manipulatees'' are merely one step lower in the pecking order of manipulators; they are being manipulated, but in turn are manipulating others less ''skilled'' at the game than they. Still, what the whole thing amounts to is that the manipulator is manipulating in order to avoid facing his own problems. Once people can be stimulated to look within themselves with courage—because it does take courage—they no longer have to manipulate. If psychologists would see the truth of this and stop playing games, they could help obviate the major cause of most of the troubles in the world, if you will let me put it that way.

I'd like you to do me a favor, Doctor. I've been nudging David with some ideas on this subject that he calls "The Game." These are mainly his ideas, but I've helped him shape them. I think he's going to type them out in the next few days. Would you get him to polish this and include it with this interview?

Leichtman: Yes, it is a beautiful allegory of what you've just been describing, expressed in symbols that are easily understood by most people.

Jung: It's not the usual way to arrive at a psychological model, but it will be helpful for the average layman—and hopefully there will be a few reading this book.

By, the way, I find it's really easy for me to "overshadow" David. I don't particularly care for that term, but we'll have to stick with it, I suppose.

Leichtman: Would you prefer "exfluence"?

[*Laughter.*]

Jung: It's more of a blending.

Leichtman: I understand the distinction.

Jung: I am going to close on that thought, and I would like to thank you for the opportunity to visit with the good Doctor this evening.

Freud: Yes. It has been a pleasure.

Leichtman: Thank you.

Freud: May I make a closing comment also? I would like to make a final plea to my colleagues to take the psychological principles that have been laid down and go forward with them, rather than being caught up in the dogma of the past interpretations of my work and Dr. Jung's work. If this can happen—if there are some psychiatrists and psychologists who will move out to the threshold of psychology, move out to the periphery and explore their own minds with the knowledge that they have—then psychology will go where it should. There will be a much more humanistic view and a much more holistic view of the human mind—the wonderful human mind as it is.

It has been wonderful to have been a part of this project.

Leichtman: I was very honored that you could come.

A TYPICAL MOVE IN "THE GAME"

THE GAME

A Psychological Model of Manipulation

by D. Kendrick Johnson

Several years ago, I realized that I was repeatedly being manipulated in personal relationships. Many of the people I dealt with would play upon my sympathies, my sense of fairness, and my good-heartedness to induce me to cooperate with their own selfish plans. I had always considered these parts of my character to be strengths, but now I was discovering, much to my chagrin, that they could be vulnerabilities. This was a problem that both annoyed and puzzled me; I could not understand why it happened or what I was doing to encourage others to use me in this way.

As my injured feelings and negative reactions mounted, however, I began to realize that I was not alone in this dilemma. I found that there are many good people like myself who do not always use their common sense and compassion to best advantage—at least, not until circumstances force them to. As a group, we assume that others respect our humanity just as we respect theirs; we deal openly and honestly with others, only to have our trust and goodwill frequently betrayed. Naively, we fail to recognize that the world is full of tricksters who are ready to take advantage of us. In this way, we expose ourselves to being manipulated—and then are emotionally hurt when we find out that our trust has indeed been abused. This leaves us in a state of bewilderment, guilt, and self doubt which makes it difficult to understand what to do next.

Eventually, I concluded that the sense of confusion that I was experiencing was actually a greater problem than the fact that I had been used. So, I decided that I needed something to help me become more objective in examining both the events and the people involved in these cases of manipulation.

To help solve this type of problem, mathematical models are sometimes constructed and then analyzed by computers. But I am an artist and not much of a mathematician. In any event, no computer was available to me. Instead, I had to devise another way of creating a model which would describe the pattern of events in which I was being used again and again. But to be effective, I knew that any such model would have to be free of my own personal feelings and reactions. Otherwise, it would not help me recognize the first signs of a recurrence of the pattern, thus enabling me to avoid it.

I suspect that the ghostly hand of Carl Jung may have assisted in the formulation of the model which I finally conceived. It resembles a chess game and is based on the principle that our universe really *is* orderly, and that the part of the universe that the manipulators of the world try so hard to control—the physical plane—is not the most important part of life. There are a number of non-physical realms which must be considered as well as the physical plane and its events, as the ability to operate at these "inner levels" gives us the only valid way of understanding and controlling the physical dimension. In this perspective, the tricksters who seem so very clever as they play their games begin to emerge as the most stupid of all.

"The Game," as I have titled my model, has worked remarkably well for me and others who have used it. It is presented here in the hope that it will stimulate the thinking of other unhappy victims of situations similar to mine.

The players in The Game all belong to one of three types: *Ah!*, *Be*, or *See!* The Game is played on a board that is laid out with an infinite number of squares. Above the baseboard are several parallel boards that duplicate, square for square, the layout of the baseboard. In this way, it resembles a three-dimensional chess board constructed in infinite dimensions.

Players move from one square to another on either the baseboard or on any combination of the upper boards. A player who is moving on the baseboard may jump up any number of levels for a series of moves, but he must return to the baseboard at some future point. Such a complex move is used when it can lead to an end which would not be possible by moving only on the baseboard. A player can also choose to remain on the upper levels for all further plays. Such a decision, however, may restrict his participation in The Game, since his plays are limited to moving in alliance with a player on the baseboard below.

Various cards are issued during the play, as rewards or penalties. Cards are issued only on the baseboard, with one exception: a card is also issued to a player upon his first jump to the upper levels. This is the *only* official card in The Game; all the rest are counterfeit!

The *Ah!* player never acts from a position of strength, and he knows this from the beginning. *Ah!* feels that even being entered in The Game is a great insult; as a result, he thinks he has the right to cheat. Moreover, he believes that he can win The Game only by cheating. *Ah!* therefore freely revises the rules at any time without notifying the other players. Eventually, he comes to believe that he is the only one who is allowed to change the rules. This kind of deception does not make him feel guilty, however, because he already has in his possession a ''guilt card'' that he counterfeited for himself during a confused fit of pique.

As a result of his frenetic activities, the rules of The Game are not clear to *Ah!* In his confusion, *Ah!* seeks to ''pass GO and collect $200.'' He is not aware, as are the *Be* players, that GO is not the object of The Game. Actually, GO is not even on the board. Not knowing this is *Ah!'s* most critical vulnerability.

Ah! is limited to playing only for the objective that he *thinks* the other players are pursuing. He has changed the rules so often for himself and others that he is confused and cannot evaluate for himself the true nature of The Game.

Be, by his very nature, has what *Ah!* lacks—an instinctive grasp of The Game. For this reason, *Be* can play The Game from a position of great strength; at the same time, however, he can also be quite naive and vulnerable. *Be* can see the true objective from the beginning of play, and he can also perceive the natural and proper moves that must be made in order to gain the objective. He likewise intuits the fact that the real rules of The Game are there to help him.

The weakness of *Be's* play is that his understanding of the rules is natural and instinctive; therefore, he does not bother to examine them *consciously*. In addition, he assumes that all other players have the same understanding and are playing by the same rules. Unlike *Ah!*, he has no interest in ''winning'' the game; because he understands the Ultimate Objective of The Game and knows that it is inherent in The Game itself, it nevers occurs to him to consider ''winning'' as a possible motive.

Ah! and *Be* meet in play. *Be* is set on the objective of The Game and assumes that *Ah!* is as well. In making any specific move, *Be* considers the point of the *whole* game as well as the move that is immediately obvious to him. *Ah!* sees that *Be* is moving and assumes that *Be's* intention is to reach GO. *Ah!* thus conjures up a strategy to outmaneuver *Be* so that he can get to the square that *Be* is moving toward before *Be* does, and capture it. *Ah!* does not want *Be* to suspect what he is doing, however, and so he tries to confuse *Be* as to his real objective—which is actually only *Ah!'s* idea of *Be's* goals. *Ah!* therefore changes the rules so that he can capture any square ''won'' by *Be* in a series of complex moves that are designed to keep *Be* from realizing that *Ah!* has found GO—which he hasn't. *Be* usually fails to perceive this deception, because he knows that GO is part of another game altogether, and is therefore inclined to ignore it.

Be moves in a direct line to whichever nearby square

leads to the natural object of The Game. He does not move defensively, because he knows that *all* players can succeed; there is no need for competitive play. As a consequence, he is totally open and honest about his plays. *Be* makes obvious, purposeful, and well-considered moves—indeed, he often announces what his next series of moves will be before making them. He does this because he realizes that the skill acquired in moving through The Game toward the Ultimate Objective is actually more important than the moves themselves. He therefore invites other players to help him in playing The Game, reasoning that through cooperation, skills can be learned more rapidly.

In his cunning, *Ah!* observes that *Be* is open and trusting, and regards him as stupid for it. *Ah!* is out to win and assumes that only one player can do so. He is determined to be that winner and thus acts competitively in all his plays. He scorns cooperation but frequently uses the appearance of it to get *Be* to reveal his intentions. He must do this because he depends on *Be* to show him the way to win. His method requires that he see *Be's* next immediate move in advance, so that he can outmaneuver his ''opponent.'' He does not have the capacity to act creatively himself.

Ah! does gain a certain tactical brilliance in his defensive moves, by appearing to make offensive ones. The way in which he gains a square may be truly dazzling. *Be* then arrives on the same square which, after all, is the one he said he was heading for in the first place. *Ah!* promptly manufactures a new set of rules so he can claim that *Be* committed a foul by landing on ''his'' square. *Ah!* consequently hands *Be* a penalty card which requires that *Be* must either go back several squares or be removed from the board. Of course, *Ah!* does not really have the authority or the power to enforce this penalty—he can get away with it only as long as *Be* mistakenly believes him to be honest. *Ah!* relies on the gullibility and quiescence that he thinks he sees in *Be*; actually, he fears *Be*'s removal from the board, as it would deprive him of a directing influence.

As The Game advances and *Be* acquires skills, he begins to realize that *Ah!* is indeed cheating. He also comprehends that he has lost a great deal due to *Ah!*'s interference. *Be* is stunned by this discovery, as he cannot understand why anyone would want to behave in this senseless fashion. As a direct result of this awakening, *Be* voluntarily skips several turns at play, so that he can have time to consciously review the nature and rules of The Game in his mind. This pause marks the first time that *Be* has deliberately tried to comprehend The Game; until now, his understanding has been instinctive and automatic.

In his confusion, *Ah!* now concludes that he has *Be* where he wants him. He believes that he is close to winning—that *Be* has stopped because he knows that he is defeated. *Ah!*, of course, never considers that *Be* has seen through him. Foolishly, he begins to hope that *Be* will indeed be removed from the board, because he is no longer useful to the now-superior *Ah!* He gloats at the prospect of being able to win in only a few more brilliant moves.

His next moves are no more brilliant than any of his earlier ones, however. Because *Ah!* has never really comprehended The Game, he is capable only of repeating or varying his previous moves. And since he is moving, he mistakenly thinks that he is still playing

The Game—and progressing. Actually, his moves are pointless. As *Be* is no longer supplying *Ah!* with goals, *Ah!* accomplishes nothing at all with his dazzling maneuvers.

It is now that The Game becomes interesting, as *Be* faces the following choices for his next moves.

Be may have become so accustomed to *Ah!*'s interference that he may conclude that it is a necessary part of The Game—an obstacle that helps him develop his strengths and skills as he seeks to neutralize it. If *Ah!* becomes aware of this, he will present *Be* with a guilt card, which *Be* will accept, believing that he has violated a part of the rules that he had overlooked. *Be* then continues to play for a few more moves, until he realizes that the guilt card is counterfeit. *Be* usually makes a major mistake at this point by throwing the guilt card away, instead of calling for an umpire.

Be may also move on for a bit until he is captured by a *See!* player. This can only happen if *Be* is still confused about why *Ah!* cheated him, because *See!*'s play in much the same manner that *Ah!*'s do. Like *Ah!*, *See!* is unaware that there is an Ultimate Objective for The Game that unites all players. He regards the other players on the board only as tools to be used for gaining control of the baseboard, which he believes to be the point of The Game.

See! is even more skilled at counterfeiting cards and confusing and using *Be*'s than *Ah!* is. *Ah!* is a bit shortsighted, usually focussing his efforts on just a single *Be*. By contrast, *See!* has discovered that the whole board is full of *Be*'s; he's worked out a way to manipulate a number of them and keep them all in a state of confusion—depending on him for continual clarification of his counterfeit rules. Of course, if *See!* ever did try to clarify a rule he had just made up, it would demonstrate even to a bewildered *Be* that he didn't know what he was doing. Like *Ah!*, *See!* can only succeed by convincing *Be* that he is honest and interested in helping *Be* with his greater wisdom and insight.

In dealing with *See!*, *Be* faces a series of moves that are similar to but more complex than the plays he has already experienced. Eventually, he will again realize that he is being cheated and will stop to think about it. That prepares him to choose another course of action.

Be may realize that none of the rules that *Ah!* and *See!* have given him applies to the real nature of The Game. He continues playing, but ignores *Ah!* and *See!* He sees the real objective once again and moves toward it, but repeats his mistake of not calling for an umpire.

While moving along the baseboard in an orderly fashion, *Be* may discover that there are several other kinds of moves he can make. Although he has not considered it before, he learns that he can at any time make broad jumps over any number of squares on the baseboard. He also discovers that he can jump to the upper levels of The Game to make a move not otherwise possible to a square on the baseboard. Both *Ah!* and *See!* consider these moves silly, and they ignore them. They aren't able to duplicate them, anyway.

On his first jump to the upper levels of the board, *Be* is presented with a Crown Card—the *only* official card that is issued in The Game. *Be* now discovers that everyone else on these upper levels is playing the same game as he, and by the same set of genuine rules.

The Game now becomes faster and simpler for *Be*, as he has learned to move on any of the upper levels and then return to any point on the baseboard. *Be* also discovers that he can receive help from those who play exclusively on the upper boards.

The more *Be* jumps to the upper levels, the sooner he learns that such jumps are necessary in order to reach the actual objective of The Game. *Ah!* and *See!* seldom grasp this truth—if they do, they are then presented with the only rule book and sent back to start The Game over again as a *Be*.

Be eventually elects to play on the upper boards exclusively. He then becomes a *BE!* and selects one or more *Be's* to help on the baseboard.

Having lost their captive *Be* player to the upper levels, *Ah!* and *See!* may get together and begin digging tunnels under the baseboard and writing graffiti on the squares. The next *Be* who comes along will have to clean up the mess.

After many tries and new beginnings, *Ah!* and *See!* eventually do learn to become *Be's*. There is always hope for them, in spite of themselves.

And that is the reason why *Be* never called an umpire.

GLOSSARY

ANCIENT WISDOM: The knowledge of the higher self; a body of teachings that is preserved at the level of the higher self and is taught by those advanced individuals who enjoy full contact with the higher self.

ARCHETYPE: A word with two distinct meanings. A *Jungian archetype* is any symbol, image, or force that is common to large numbers of people. Jungian archetypes have their existence in the personal unconscious of individuals and in the collective unconscious of humanity. While they cannot be comprehended in their totality, their influences can be recognized in one's thoughts, feelings, and intuitions. A *divine archetype* is a pattern or ideal of creation. Divine archetypes are found at the abstract levels of the mental plane, and are used by the higher self as it creates the personality, its destiny, and its behavior. This second type of archetype is also used by non-human intelligences (such as the Deva kingdom) in creating non-human forms and conditions. In this book, the word "archetype" is used only to refer to Jungian archetypes.

ASTRAL PLANE: The plane of emotions and desires. The astral plane is an inner world or plane of existence made of matter that is more subtle than physical substance, and yet it interpenetrates all physical substance. It is teeming with life of its own. The astral plane is the environment in which telepathy, imagination, and much psychic phenomena occur. It also provides the substance for astral bodies of all physical life forms.

ASTROLOGY: The science of the interplay of cosmic energies. Astronomy is the science of the interrelationship of physical bodies and energies in the universe; astrology is the science of the interrelationship of *all* bodies and forces in the cosmos—astral, mental, and even more rarefied ones, as well as physical.

CLAIRVOYANCE: The capacity to see or know beyond the limits of the physical senses—in the realms of etheric, astral, or mental existence. There are many degrees of clairvoyance, which allows an individual to comprehend forces, beings, and objects of the inner worlds normally invisible to the average person.

CLAIRVOYANT: Someone who has the faculty of clairvoyance. There are many levels of competence and many varieties of specialty among clairvoyants.

COLLECTIVE UNCONSCIOUS: The mass of symbols, images, ideas, forces, and feelings that have accumulated during the history of the entire human race. These universal forces influence our unconscious minds, but can be indirectly inferred by an intelligent person.

CONSCIOUS MIND: That portion of the mind

that is deliberately used by the personality to focus on ideas, events, and facts from moment to moment. It is the outermost tip of human awareness.

DESTINY: The combined plans and commitments that have been made by an individual's higher self for its future. A destiny would include plans for becoming creative, for achieving enlightenment, and for building specific relationships. It is not imposed from without, but is rather the product of decisions made by the self.

DEVA KINGDOM: A separate kingdom of life forms whose function and evolution is different than mankind's, although the two kingdoms are related. In ascending order, the Deva kingdom includes nature spirits, angels, and archangels. In Sanskrit, the word ''deva'' means ''celestial being.'' The Devas influence all human beings, even though they are invisible to the average eye.

DISCARNATE: A human being without a physical body, living on the inner planes. Discarnates are also known as spirit entities or ''spooks.'' This is the state of human life in between physical lives.

DIVINATION: The act of discerning the divine order of events and forces in the universe and relating it to individual self expression.

DWELLER ON THE THRESHOLD: The sumtotal of the forces of the personality. Occultly, the Dweller embodies all the psychic, emotional, and mental forces, desires, fears, and habits which have unfolded during the personal history of any one individual, including all his past incarnations and existences. The term is especially used to refer to the unredeemed aspects of these elements. In psychological terms, the Dweller on the Threshold would be a personified aspect of an individual's total personal unconscious.

HIGHER SELF: The animating principle in human consciousness—the inner being or soul. It is the guiding intelligence of the personality, the part of the human mind that is immortal.

HYPNOSIS: A psychological technique for communicating more directly (and sometimes more forcefully) with the subconscious of an individual. It is an artificial technique which does not make contact with the higher self or soul of the individual, and is therefore limited in its usefulness.

I CHING: The Chinese Book of Changes. In popular use, it is a system of divination that uses pictograms and associated commentaries that are selected by the "random" fall of coins or sticks. Its purpose is to indicate the significance of any given event or condition, rather than reveal the future.

INCARNATE: A person living with a body on the physical plane.

INITIATE: A person who has dedicated himself to a specific temple, organization, or brotherhood, and has received certain teachings, ideas, or secrets that help him fulfill his responsibilities as a member of that group. Esoterically, an initiate is a person who has dedicated his personality to the life of the higher self, and has received new wisdom, maturity, and intuitive talents so that he will be better able to fulfill the creative intent of the higher self. An initiation lets a person *begin* to consciously work with aspects of the soul.

INNER PLANES: A term used to refer to any one of several inner worlds or levels of existence, all of which interpenetrate the dense physical plane. Each physical human being exists on these inner planes as well as on the physical level, by dint of having "bodies" composed of matter drawn from them. Most human beings do not consciously use these inner bodies, however. They either operate subconsiously or are partially inactive—until activated by personal growth and the development of intuitive awareness. In general, the inner planes are considered more spiritualized than the physical. Most important events in the physical plane are directed from the inner planes.

KABALAH: A system of esoteric philosophy associated with Jewish tradition but probably predating known historical records. Rather than being a collection of dogma, the Kabalah is a system of images and symbols which relates the formless and unmanifest aspects of God with the structure of manifest creation. Its central symbol is the "Tree of Life."

MEDITATION: An act of mental rapport in which the ideals, purposes, and intents of the higher self are discerned, interpreted, and applied by the personality. To be meaningful, meditation must be a very active state in which creative ideas, new realizations, and inspirations are pursued with vigor. The current belief that meditation is a passive state of emptying the mind, by concentrating on a mantra or by just "sitting," is the antithesis of true meditation.

MEDIUM: A person who practices mediumship by conscious choice.

MEDIUMSHIP: The phenomenon of a non-physical intelligence, usually a discarnate human, assuming some degree of control of a physical body in order to communicate something useful and meaningful. Mediumship is usually used for the transmission of information or inspired guidance, but can also be used to transmit varieties of healing energies. There are varying degrees of trance associated with mediumship and differing qualities of information communicated, depending on the quality of the medium and the quality of the spirit using the process. Mediumship is distinguished from the phenomenon of possession in that it occurs only with the deliberate cooperation of the medium and produces a constructive result.

MENTAL HOUSECLEANING: The process of organizing and disciplining the mind and its contents: thoughts, attitudes, convictions, habits, and feelings. This work is a necessary part of attaining and preserving mental health, just as physical housecleaning is a necessary part of keeping one's living quarters neat, clean, and livable. When mental housecleaning is ignored, conditions of psychological illness can occur, which then require the attention of therapy, psychoanalysis, or psychiatric counseling. The goal of mental housecleaning is to put in order and cleanse one's subconscious associations, beliefs, and behavior patterns. This process is most effective when authority for it is given to the higher self.

META-ARCHETYPE: A term used by Dr. Jung in this conversation to refer to a thought-form that is common to large numbers of people. It has its existence in the astral plane but is created by the imaginings or fears of unenlightened people. Thus, it is dependent upon the conscious thoughts of people. The true Jungian archetype, on the other hand, has an existence that is *not* dependent on people, even though humanity is influenced by them.

MIND: The portion of the human personality that has the capacity to think. The mind is an organized field of energy that exists in invisible dimensions. It is *not* the physical brain, although it does operate through the brain during physical life.

MIND PARASITE: A term coined by Colin Wilson in his novel, *The Mind Parasites.* A mind parasite is a denizen of the astral plane that thrives on the unpleasant thoughts of mankind. It can be either an elemental life form that has been taught bad habits by association with human beings, or a thought entity created entirely by a human being which then attacks its creator. In either case, mind parasites feed on the depression, anguish, hatred, and vulgar thoughts of men and women and seek to increase them. When their parasitism is threatened by an intelligent person who seeks to educate others about the dangers of depression, anger, and vulgarity, they will mentally attack that individual and try to disrupt his mental stability. Occultly, they are known as vampires. Many psychological disorders are fed by the invisible activities of mind parasites.

MYSTICISM: The process of loving, revering, and *finding* God and His entire Creation.

MYTH: A symbolic story that explains some mystery of human nature—its origin, its purpose, or its destiny. The current belief that myths are by nature false is itself a falsehood. For a story to be considered a myth, it must symbolically reveal some important truth about life. Therefore, myths are rich sources for study by psychologists.

OCCULT: The hidden secrets of nature. The study of the occult deals not just with the esoteric aspects of man's being, but also the entire universe. It includes the study of the function, operation, purpose, origin, and destiny of nature and man. The word "occult" literally means "that which is hidden."

OCCULTIST: One who studies the secrets of nature and the invisible patterns of order in life.

PARAPSYCHIC: A term used by Dr. Jung in this conversation to refer exclusively to the aspect of the human mind that is capable of being telepathic, clairvoyant, or intuitive. It means exactly the same thing as the normal usage of the word "psychic."

PARAPSYCHOLOGY: The study of psychic phenomena.

PERSONAL UNCONSCIOUS: The unconscious thoughts, habits, urges, and feelings that influence an individual human being.

PERSONALITY: That part of a human being that is used for manifestation in the earth plane. It is composed of a mind, a set of emotions, and a physical body, each containing conscious and subconscious functions. It is the child of the higher self and its experiences on earth.

PRECOGNITION: The ability to foresee a future event before it happens.

PSYCHE: Human consciousness. In Greek mythology, Psyche is the personification of the human soul.

PSYCHIC: In general usage, a person who is able to perceive events and information without the use of the physical senses. The word is also used to refer to any event associated with the phenomena of parapsychology. However, Freud, Jung, and many psychologists use the word as an adjectival form of "psyche," to refer to *any* expression of thought or feeling.

PSYCHIC ATTACK: A telepathic attack from the subconscious of another person or from a mind parasite. Any expression of anger, hatred, envy, malice, intimidation, or severe possessiveness is a psychic attack that can be felt by the object of the attack and others around him, even though it is seldom recognized as such. A psychic attack is an assault upon the mind and the emotions, and can be far more severe than many physical assaults. This phenomenon is a major factor in psychological disturbances.

REINCARNATION: The concept that the higher self evolves through a successive and progressive series of different physical personalities. The higher self finds it convenient and most practical to use a sequence of different personalities, covering millions of years, to fulfill its ultimate purpose. Reincarnation should not be mistaken for ''transmigration,'' a spurious doctrine that suggests that human entities can return in future lives as different kinds of animals. Reincarnation refers only to the use by the higher self of successive human personalities to achieve mastery.

REPRESSION: The act of unconsciously forgetting something that is unpleasant. The repressed memory does not totally vanish, however; it is stored as a bad seed in the unconscious, and will tend to reappear in one form or another.

SABIAN SYMBOLS: A series of 360 symbols derived by Marc Edmund Jones and a psychic, Miss Elsie Wheeler, in 1925. The symbols represent the key meaning of specific degrees of the zodiac and are used by some astrologers in interpreting horoscopes. The term ''Sabian'' comes from the name of the group Jones led, the Sabian Assembly. These symbols have been popularized by the writings of astrologer Dane Rudhyar—most notably in *The Astrology of Personality* and *An Astrological Mandala*.

[95]

SEANCE: The event of a discarnate spirit entity speaking through a medium, in order to communicate with physical people.

SECRET ENTRANCE TO THE MIND: The mental doorway in a medium's mind through which a spirit entity can enter.

SELF: A psychological term used by Dr. Jung to describe the center of the totality of both the unconscious and conscious aspects of the mind. It functions to unite and integrate the diverse elements of the mind. The human mind often personifies the self so that it may be experienced symbolically in dreams, meditations, and so on.

SHADOW: A Jungian term for the personalized part of one's personal unconscious. It contains repressed memories and much of the uncivilized or negative aspects of the personality—but also contains the creative capacity of the individual.

SMALL INTELLIGENCES: The term used by Dr. Jung in this interview to refer to the most primitive inhabitants of the astral and mental planes. In occult terms, these beings would be called "elementals."

SPOOK: An affectionate term for a discarnate.

SUBCONSCIOUS: The part of the personality that is not being consciously used at any given moment. The subconscious is always active and greatly influences our conscious moods, thoughts, acts, and attitudes. It is psychically in tune with other portions of the inner planes—even if we are not consciously psychic at all.

SUPPRESSION: The deliberate effort to ignore something that is unpleasant. A suppressed memory cannot be totally ignored, however; it is stored as a bad seed in the subconscious and the unconscious, and will tend to reappear in one form or another.

SYMBOL: An image, thought, feeling, or event that contains a deeper significance than what is obvious from the outer form. It points to inner dimensions of reality, force, and meaning. To discern these inner dimensions, however, the symbol must be interpreted. The study of symbolism is useful only if it leads to a discovery of the reality that the symbol veils.

TAROT CARDS: A species of cards, each card featuring a symbolic portrayal of an esoteric quality or force. Sometimes used in fortune telling and divination, the esoteric purpose of Tarot cards is to provide an allegorical key to the structure of life. By studying and using the Tarot, one can gain knowledge of the hidden aspects of nature. It is interconnected with certain aspects of the Kabalah, astrology, and alchemy.

TELEPATHIC: A condition of direct mind-to-mind communication, without using physical signals.

THOUGHT-FORM: Literally, the form that one's thoughts take on the plane on which they are created, usually the astral or mental. Visible only to a clairvoyant, thought-forms are nonetheless created by every human being during the ordinary process of thinking and feeling. Each person is influenced by thought-forms and influences others with the ones he creates. A thought-form embodies the quality, strength, and definition of the astral or thought matter from which it was shaped.

TRANCE: A state in which ordinary consciousness is quieted so that another element of consciousness can use the physical voicebox and body. In a hypnotic or drug-induced trance, the subconscious assumes control

[97]

of the body. In a mediumistic trance, another entity takes over. A trance state often seems to resemble sleeping but is actually much different: the physical body remains responsive and can be used actively.

UNCONSCIOUS: The part of the mind not ordinarily accessible to the conscious mind. It is filled in part with repressed memories, desires, fears, and feelings that are usually glimpsed only in dreams or in automatic behavior, such as "slips of the tongue." This is the part that psychologists have usually dealt with. But there are other parts to the unconscious as well: the seeds of noble, enlightened qualities, creative impulses, memories of experiences from earlier lives and existences, and an awareness of other life forms.

VAMPIRISM: The phenomenon of sapping or stealing energy from another individual through a telepathic or psychic contact. It is a common feature of sexual abnormalities, but is found in other contexts as well.

WITCHCRAFT: A debased form of occultism, in which the goal is to manipulate physical and astral energy for the purposes of the personality. The goal of true occultism, by contrast, is to advance the life of the spirit. Witchcraft, therefore, is the exact opposite of occultism.

FROM HEAVEN TO EARTH

The complete series of 12 interviews is available by subscription for $27 (for overseas delivery, $30). Each interview is published as a paperback book such as this one.

The spirits interviewed are Edgar Cayce, William Shakespeare, Cheiro, Carl Jung and Sigmund Freud, C.W. Leadbeater, Sir Oliver Lodge, Thomas Jefferson, Arthur Ford, H.P. Blavatsky, Nikola Tesla, Eileen Garrett, and Stewart White. All 12 books are now in print.

Orders can be placed by sending a check for the proper amount to Ariel Press, 3391 Edenbrook Court, Columbus, Ohio 43220. Please make checks payable, in U.S. funds, to Ariel Press, or charge to MasterCard, VISA, or American Express. Ohio residents should add 5½ % sales tax.

Individual copies of the interviews are also available, at $3.50 plus $1 postage each, when ordered from the publisher. When 10 or more copies of a *single* title are ordered, the cost is $2.50 per book plus the actual cost of shipping.

These books may also be purchased through your favorite bookstore.

ACTIVE MEDITATION

Meditation is a set of practices which help us bring the life and power of the higher self into expression in the daily activities of the personality. The regular use of meditation enriches consciousness, illumines the mind, increases self-discipline, stimulates creativity, and integrates the personality with the higher self.

Effective meditation has been part of every significant spiritual tradition in human history—because there is no better way of establishing contact between the personality and the higher self. And yet, not all systems of meditation lead to enlightenment. In many systems, the art of meditation has been trivialized. Instead of serving as a method for establishing contact with the higher self, it has become a simple process of relaxing or quieting the mind and body. Many people accept these practices as legitimate aspects of meditation, but they are not.

Active Meditation: The Western Tradition sets the record straight. Written by Robert R. Leichtman, M.D. and Carl Japikse, it is a comprehensive examination of the tradition, purpose, potential, and techniques of meditation. More importantly, it is a masterful statement of the emerging Western tradition of personal and spiritual growth. It is a book which challenges, inspires, enlightens, and informs.

The tone set by Dr. Leichtman and Mr. Japikse emphasizes the practical nature of meditation. To them, the subjects of meditation and personal growth are inseparable—the work of meditation should always be connected with the development of a greater capacity to act wisely and creatively in the physical plane.

Active Meditation: The Western Tradition is therefore something more than just a precise definition of the art of meditation. It is also a thorough commentary on personal and spiritual growth. In specific, the authors describe:

- What meditation is—and is not.
- How meditation accelerates growth.
- The nature of the higher self.
- How to contact the higher self.
- The work of integration.
- The skills of meditation and how to use them.
- Seven specific techniques of Active Meditation.
- Meditating to help others.
- Group meditations.

Throughout, the constant goal of the authors is to strip away the vagueness and obscurity often associated with meditation and treat their subject with common sense, clarity, detailed explanations, and good humor. *Active Meditation: The Western Tradition* is easy to read and understand—and yet has also been acclaimed as *the* standard reference book on meditation. In many ways, it is the most encyclopedic book ever written on the subject, filled with information vital to everyone who meditates—and everyone interested in personal and spiritual growth.

Active Meditation: The Western Tradition is 512 pages, hardbound, and includes a glossary and index. It can be purchased at all leading bookstores or directly from Ariel Press for $24.50 plus $1.50 for postage ($2.50 outside of the U.S.). To order, send a check or money order in U.S. funds to Ariel Press, 3391 Edenbrook Court, Columbus, Ohio 43220.

THE PRIESTS OF GOD

Due to the popularity of the first series of 12 books in *From Heaven to Earth*, a second series of 12 interviews has also been conducted by Dr. Robert R. Leichtman and is now fully in print.

The spirits interviewed in this second series are all individuals who demonstrated a remarkable capacity to act with genius, leadership, and inspiration in their respective fields. The 12 spirits are Albert Schweitzer, Rembrandt, Sir Winston Churchill, Paramahansa Yogananda, Mark Twain, Albert Einstein, Benjamin Franklin, Andrew Carnegie, Richard Wagner, Luther Burbank, and Abraham Lincoln. The final book, *The Destiny of America*, is an interview with a number of famous American leaders: Alexander Hamilton, Thomas Jefferson, Benjamin Franklin, Franklin Delano Roosevelt, Harry Truman, Theodore Roosevelt, and George Washington.

The cost of subscribing to all 12 books is $27, postpaid. Orders can be placed by sending a check for the proper amount to Ariel Press, 3391 Edenbrook Court, Columbus, Ohio 43220. Make checks payable to Ariel Press. Orders can also be charged to MasterCard, VISA, or American Express. In Ohio, please add 5 ½ % sales tax.

Individual copies of the interviews are available at $3.50 plus $1 postage each. If 10 or more copies of *a single title* are ordered at one time, the price is $2.50 a book plus the actual costs of shipping.